Table of Contents

Module 19 1
Module 20 17
Module 21 39
Module 22 48
Module 23 59
Module 24 68
Module 25 84
Module 26 91
Module 27 98
Module 28 103
Module 29 113
Module 30 121
Module 32 129
Module 33 138
Module 34 152
Module 35 168
Module 36 185
Cutout Worksheets 193
Extra Resources 290

This workbook contains all of the worksheets found in the Math 2 Semester B course. To see the worksheet in color, view it online within the lessons. For any worksheets containing cutting activities, they can be found in the "Cutout Worksheets" section. The "Extra Resources" contain helpful tools that students are learning to use.

© 2021 by Accelerate Education
Visit us on the Web at www.accelerate.education

Name: _____ Date: _____

Number Line
Can you use this number line to find the sum?

74 + 22 =

← | | | | | | | | | | | | | | | | | | | | | | | | | | | | | | | →
70 71 72 73 74 75 76 77 78 79 80 81 82 83 84 85 86 87 88 89 90 91 92 93 94 95 96 97 98 99 100

19.1 Sums Using a Number Line

Name: _____ Date: _____

Sums Using a Number Line

Use these number lines to find the sums.

Example:

94 + 14 = 108

1 ten   4 ones

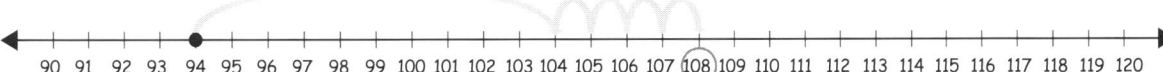

23 + 44 = ___

__ tens   __ ones

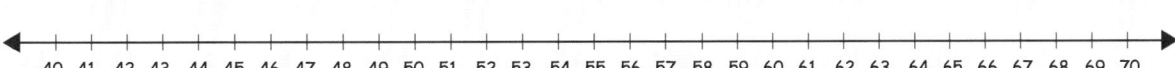

77 + 29 = ___

__ tens   __ ones

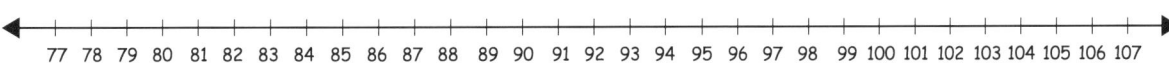

19.1 Sums Using a Number Line

Next page

93 + 22 = ___

__ tens __ ones

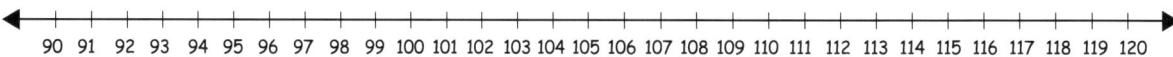

100 + 30 = ___

__ tens __ ones

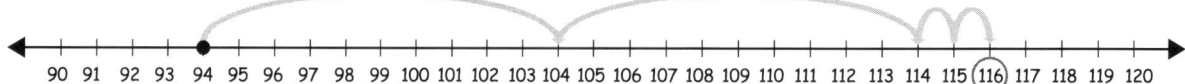

Which number line helps you solve this addition sentence?

26 + 94 = ___

__ tens __ ones

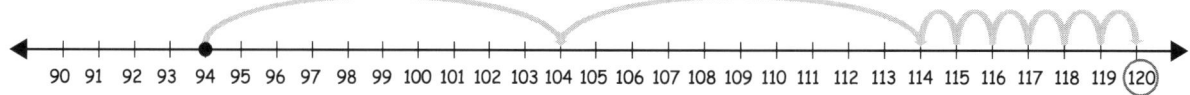

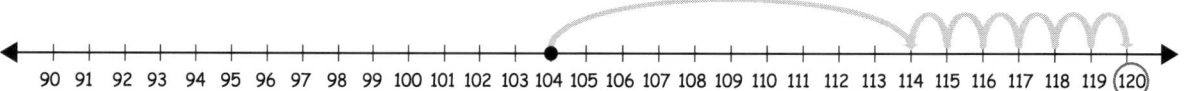

Name: _____ Date: _____

Number Line
Use this number line to solve this word problem.

Charlie has super strength. He used his left hand to lift a bookshelf that was 23 pounds. He used his right hand to lift a table that was 49 pounds. How many pounds did Charlie lift altogether?

☐ + ☐ = ☐

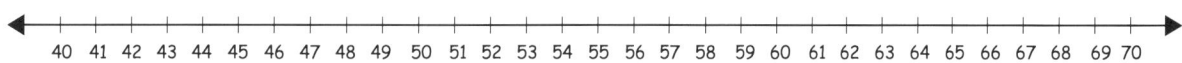

19.2 Solve Word Problems by Adding

4

Name: _____ Date: _____

Solve Word Problems by Adding

Can you solve word problems about Tiny Turtle using a number line? Write the addends and sum in the blank addition sentence, and use the number line to show your work.

Example:

Tiny Turtle ran 25 feet to a rabbit. Then he ran another 12 feet to the finish line. How many feet did Tiny Turtle run altogether?

25 + 12 = 37

1 ten   2 ones

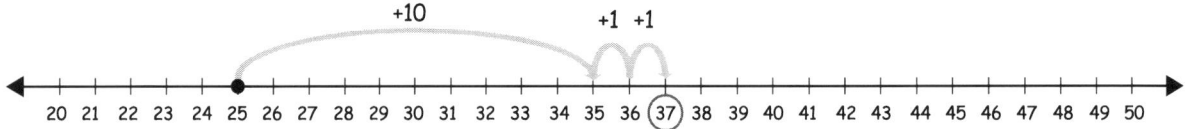

Tiny Turtle walked for 60 minutes and stopped for a snack. Then he walked another 18 minutes and stopped for a drink of water. How many minutes did Tiny Turtle walk?

60 + 18 = ___

___ ten   ___ ones

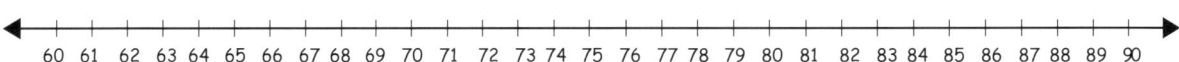

Tiny Turtle had been running for 45 yards when he saw a golden coin. He ran another 21 yards to the golden coin. How many yards did Tiny Turtle run?

45 + 21 = ___

__ ten __ ones

13 seconds has passed, and Tiny Turtle is running as fast as he can. He's able to run for another 33 seconds before taking a break. How many seconds did Tiny Turtle run?

33 + 13 = ___

__ ten __ ones

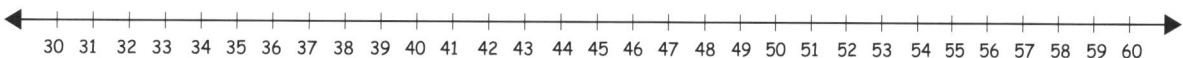

Tiny Turtle walked 24 feet. He saw his friend James and walked another 76 feet. How many feet did Tiny Turtle walk altogether?

76 + 24 = ___

__ ten __ ones

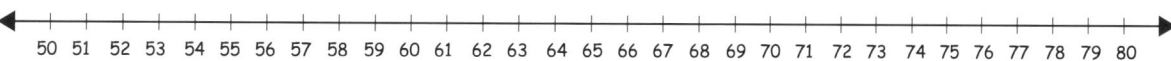

Tiny Turtle ran 55 miles at super speed. He walked another 16 miles to cool down. How many miles did Tiny Turtle go in total?

55 + 16 = ___

__ ten __ ones

19.2 Solve Word Problems by Adding

Name: _____ Date: _____

Number Line

Can you use this number line to find the difference?

120 - 25 = ☐

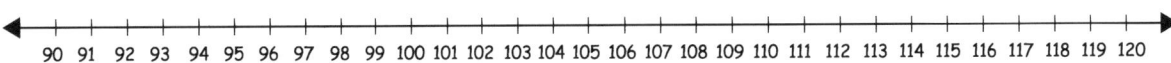

7   19.3 Differences Using A Number Line

Name: _____ Date: _____

Differences Using a Number Line

Can you find the differences using these number lines?

Example:

45 - 23 = 22
↙ ↘
2 tens   3 ones

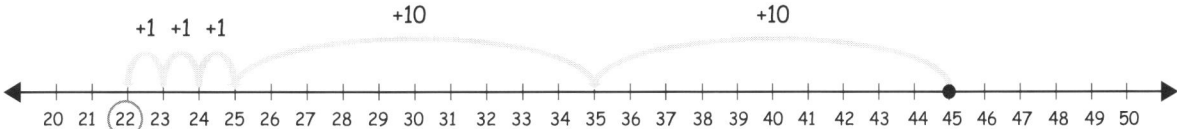

32 - 27 = ___
↙ ↘
__ tens   __ ones

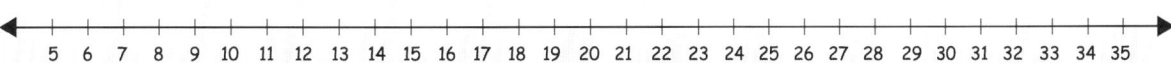

66 - 13 = ___
↙ ↘
__ tens   __ ones

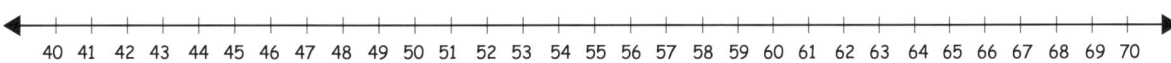

19.3 Differences Using A Number Line

8

Next page

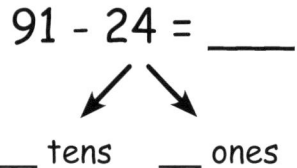

___ tens ___ ones

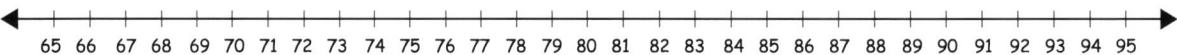

___ tens ___ ones

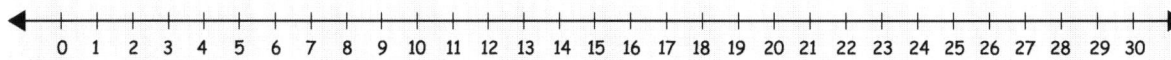

Which subtraction sentence matches each number line below?
Write the letter next to each number line.

      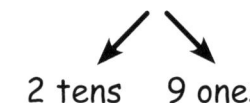

3 tens 0 one   1 ten 7 ones   2 tens 9 ones

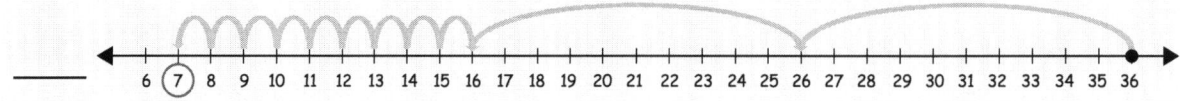

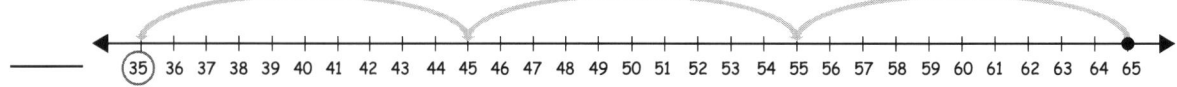

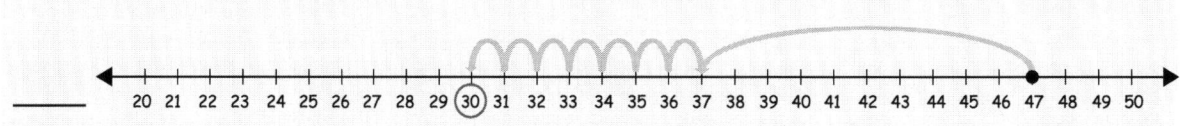

19.3 Differences Using A Number Line

Name: _____ Date: _____

Number Lines
Practice adding and subtracting on these number lines.

65 + 6 =

82 + 4 =

19.4 Number Lines

10

Name: _____ Date: _____

Number Lines
Let's practice using open number lines to add and subtract!

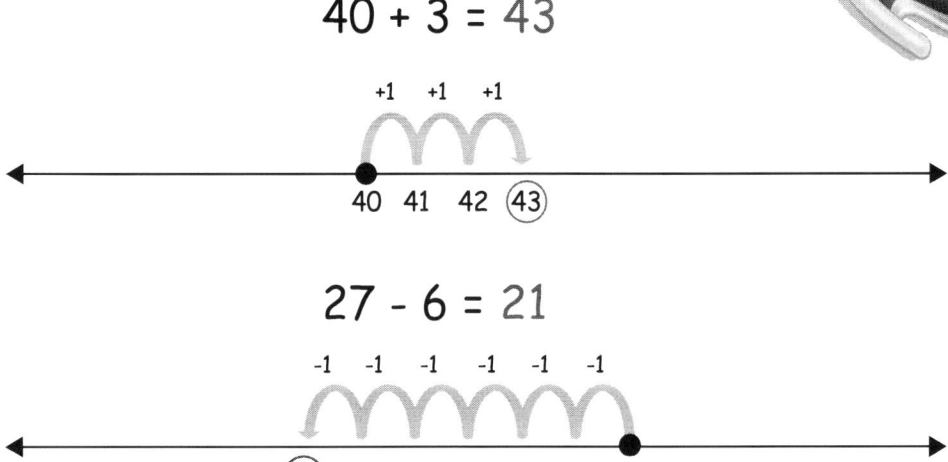

Examples:

40 + 3 = 43

27 - 6 = 21

Draw jumps to add and subtract. Write the answers in the blanks.

72 + 7 = ___

+1 +1 +1 +1 +1 +1 +1

72 73 74 75 76 77 78 ___

43 - 1 = ___

-1

___ 43

11

19.4 Number Lines

Next page

Draw jumps to add and subtract. Write the answers in the blanks.

$$55 + 5 = \underline{}$$

+_ +_ +_ +_ +_

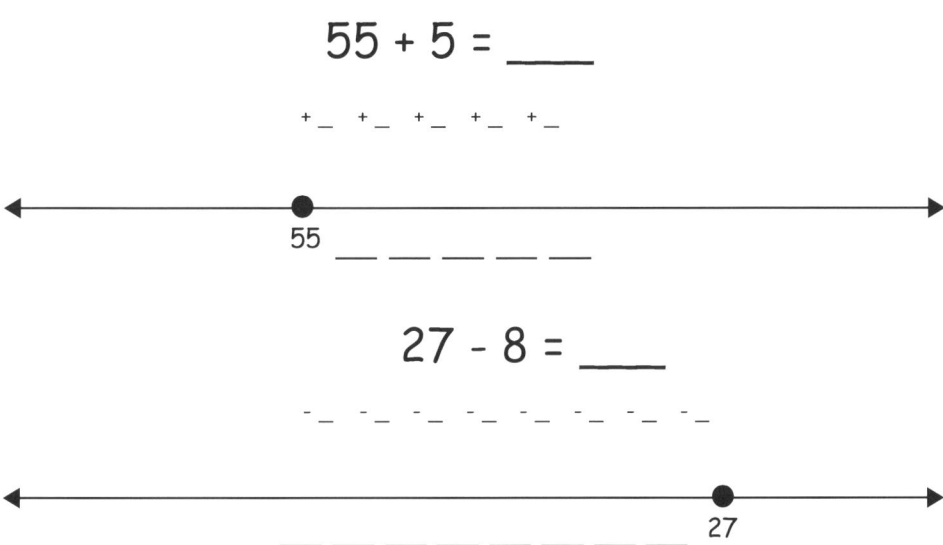

$$27 - 8 = \underline{}$$

-_ -_ -_ -_ -_ -_ -_ -_

Use these open number lines to add and subtract.

$$36 + 2 = \underline{}$$

$$64 - 6 = \underline{}$$

19.4 Number Lines

Name: _____ Date: _____

Number Line

Use this number line to solve this word problem.

Krista picked 86 blueberries. She ate 19. How many blueberries does Krista have left?

☐ - ☐ = ☐

←|—|—|—|—|—|—|—|—|—|—|—|—|—|—|—|—|—|—|—|—|—|—|—|—|—|—|—|—|—|—|→
   60 61 62 63 64 65 66 67 68 69 70 71 72 73 74 75 76 77 78 79 80 81 82 83 84 85 86 87 88 89 90

13   19.5 Solve Word Problems by Subtracting

Name: _____ Date: _____

Solve Word Problems by Subtracting

Use these number lines to solve the word problems below.

Example:

Max had 59 golf balls. 14 rolled away. How many golf balls does Max have left?

59 - 14 = 45

1 ten   4 ones

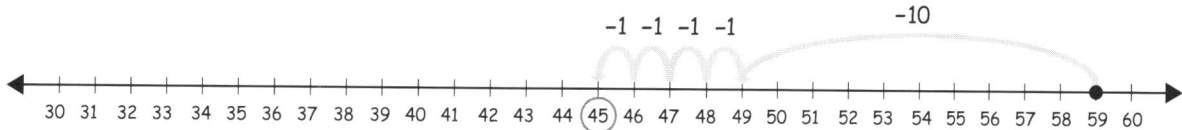

A rabbit had 33 carrots. He ate 12 of them. How many carrots does the rabbit have left?

33 - 12 = ___

___ tens   ___ ones

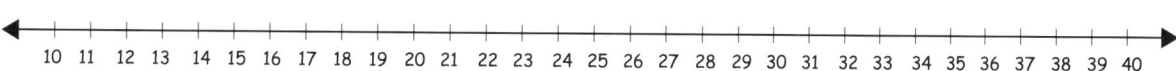

19.5 Solve Word Problems by Subtracting

Jenny climbed 95 feet up a ladder. Then she climbed 30 feet back down. How many feet is Jenny from the ground?

95 - 30 = ___

__ tens __ ones

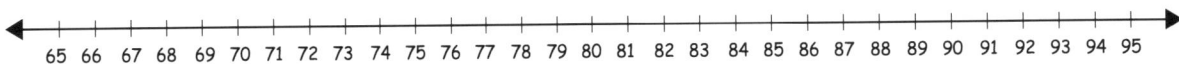

A turtle walked 25 miles in March. He walked 37 miles in April. How many more miles did the turtle walk in April than March?

37 - 25 = ___

__ tens __ ones

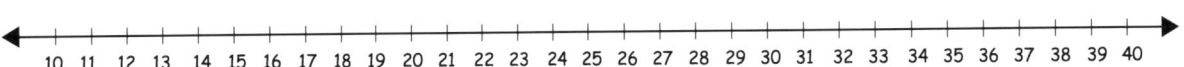

Aria was carrying 67 apples in a bucket. She dropped 21 apples. How many apples does Aria have left?

67 - 21 = ___

__ tens __ ones

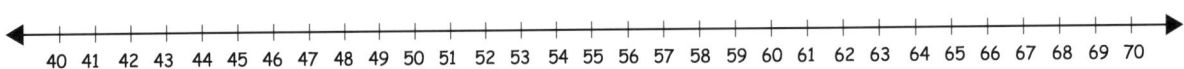

19.5 Solve Word Problems by Subtracting

Which subtraction sentence matches the number lines below?
Write the letter next to each number line.

a.

Beck checked out 28 books from the library. He is already read 11 of them. How many books does Beck have left to read?

28 - 11 = ___

b.

Jenna bought 73 candies at the store. She and her brother ate 24 candies. How many candies does Jenna have left?

73 - 24 = ___

c.

Olivia has 65 toys, and Mia has 26. How many more toys does Olivia have than Mia?

65 - 26 = ___

_____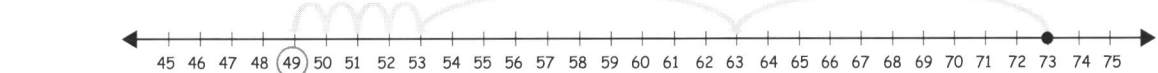

_____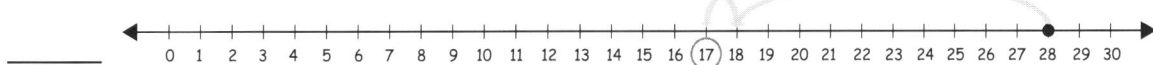

_____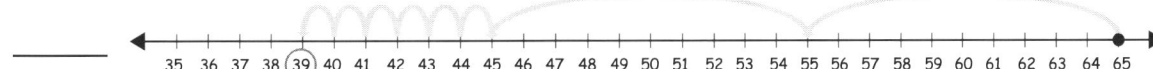

19.5 Solve Word Problems by Subtracting

Name: _____ Date: _____

Graphing Paper
Use this page to collect data and make a bar graph.

Pets	Tally Marks
Dog	
Cat	
Rabbit	
Fish	

20.1 Using Graphs to Measure

Using Graphs to Measure

Amelia collected data from her classmates about their favorite animals. Here is her data:

20.1 Using Graphs to Measure

18

Next page

Can you use Amelia's data to create a tally chart? Draw tallies for each animal.

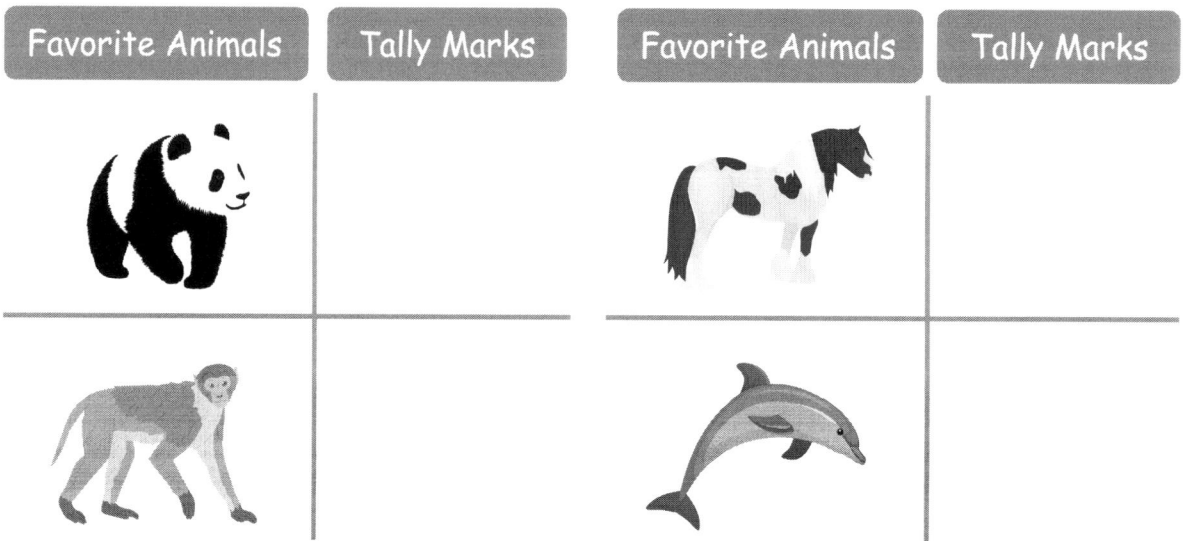

Use your tally chart to add bars to this bar graph. Use a different color to color in the bar above each animal.

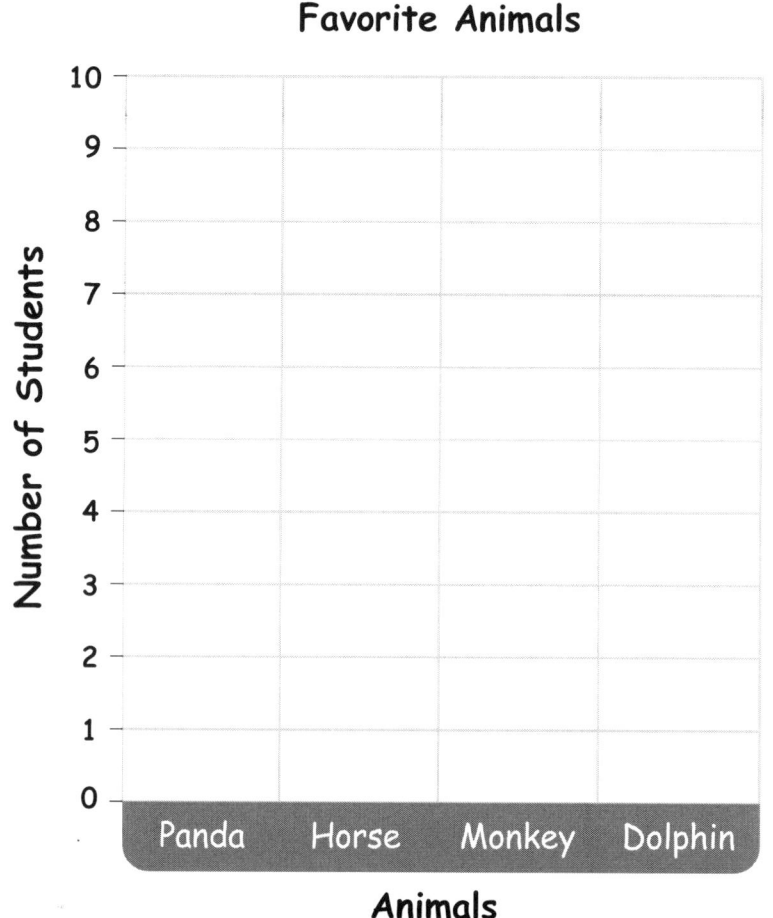

20.1 Using Graphs to Measure

Name: _____ Date: _____

Graphing Paper
Use this page to make a pictograph and a bar graph.

Seasons	Tally Marks
Summer	
Winter	
Fall	
Spring	

◆ = _____

20.2 Favorite Season Data Collection

Next page

Name: _____ Date: _____

Favorite Season Data Collection

Jenna is a second-grade student in Paris, France. She collected data from her classmates about the seasons. Can you use Jenna's data to create a tally chart? Draw a tally mark for each season.

Data

21   20.2 Favorite Season Data Collection

Next page

Tally Chart

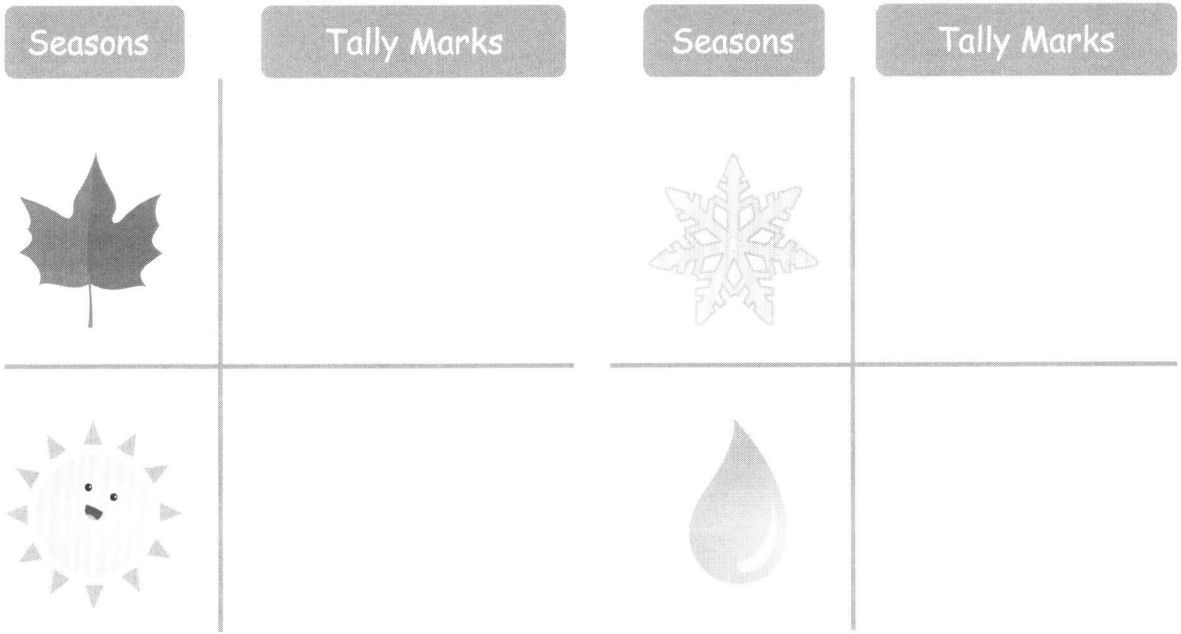

Use your tally chart to add circles to this pictograph.
Each circle equals 2 students.

Favorite Seasons	
Fall	
Winter	
Spring	
Summer	

 = 2 Students

20.2 Favorite Season Data Collection

Use your tally chart and your pictograph to add bars to this bar graph. Use different colors to color in the bars above each season.

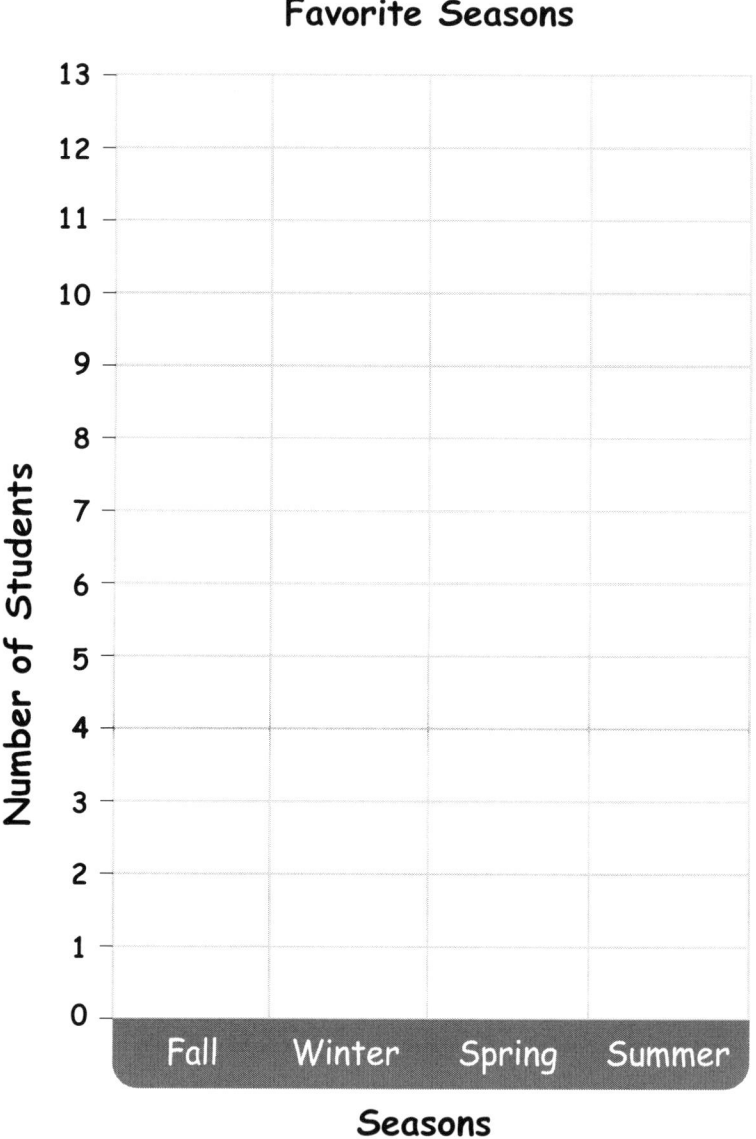

23 20.2 Favorite Season Data Collection

Name: _____ Date: _____

Graphing Paper

Use this page to make a pictograph and a bar graph.

Favorite Pizza Toppings	
Pineapple	
Tomato	
Cheese	
Pepperoni	
Mushroom	

△ 2 = Classmates

20.3 Favorite Pizza Topping Data Collection

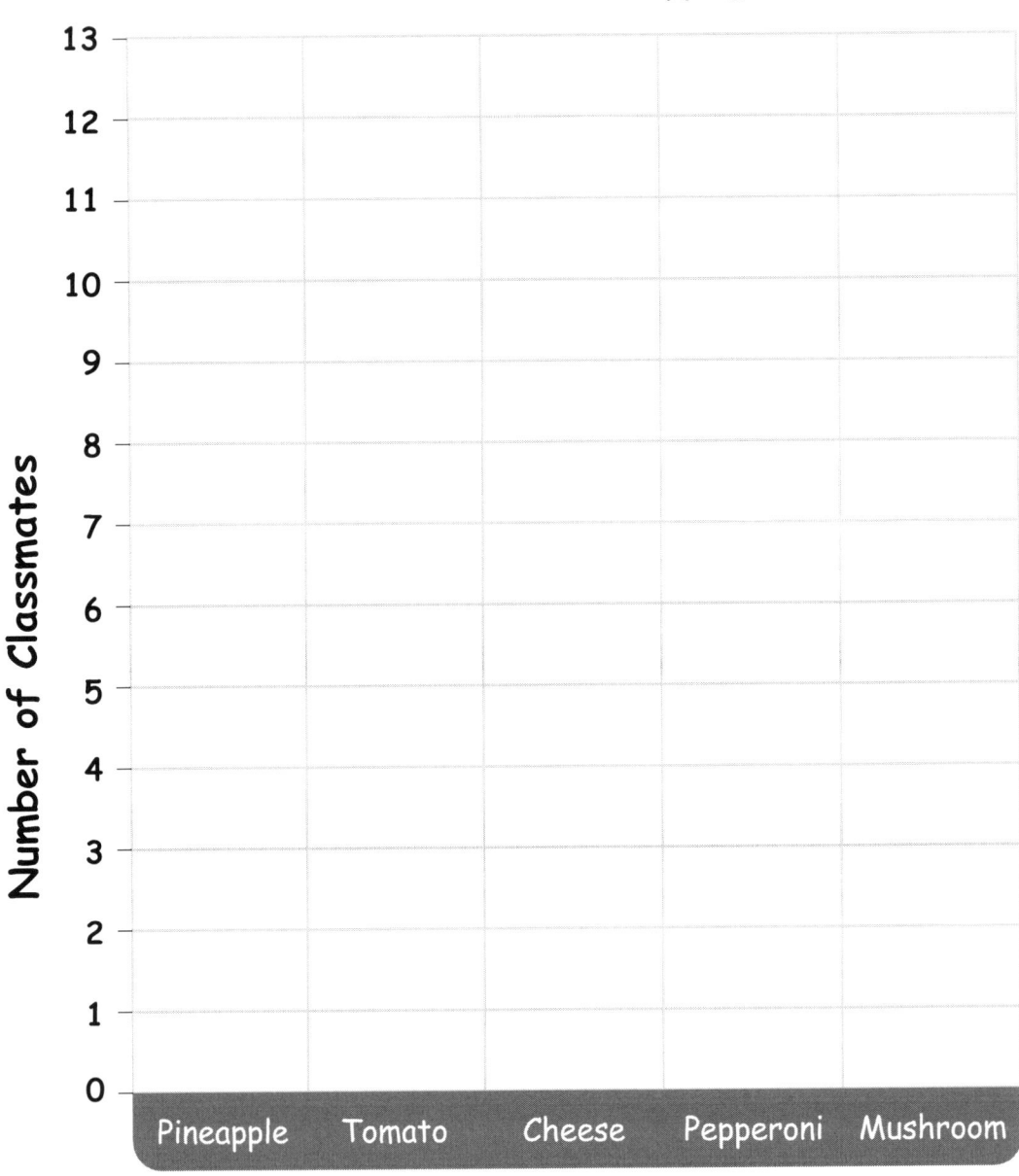

Name: _____ Date: _____

Favorite Pizza Topping Data Collection

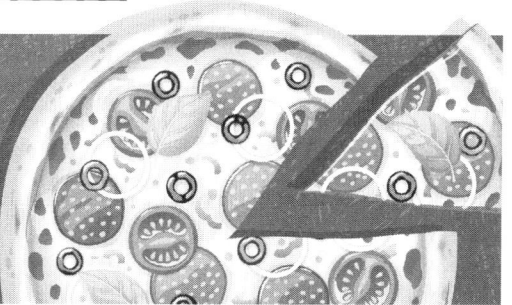

These are the graphs we created using Kira's pizza data. Let's practice using addition and subtraction to answer these questions.

Favorite Pizza Toppings	
Pineapple	▲ ▲
Tomato	▲ ▲ ▲
Cheese	▲ ▲ ▲ ▲ ▲
Pepperoni	▲ ▲ ▲ ▲ ▲ ▲ ▲
Mushroom	▲

▲ 2 = Classmates

20.3 Favorite Pizza Topping Data Collection

26

Next page

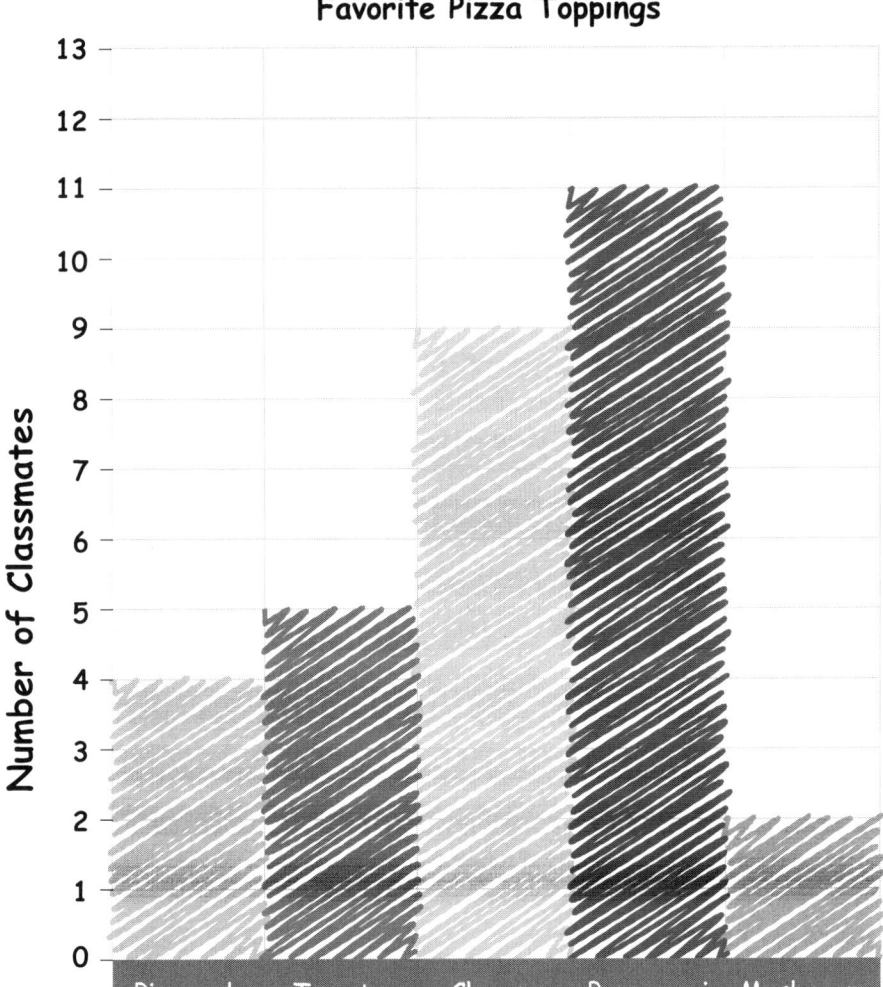

1. How many classmates voted for pepperoni and cheese as their favorite toppings? Use addition to help you find the answer.

   ___ + ___ = ___

2. How many more classmates like cheese on their pizza than like pineapple? Use subtraction to help you find the answer.

   ___ - ___ = ___

3. How many classmates like tomatoes and pineapple on their pizza? Use addition to help you find the answer.

   ___ + ___ = ___

20.3 Favorite Pizza Topping Data Collection

4. How many classmates like pineapple, tomatoes, and mushrooms on their pizza? Use addition to help you find the answer.

   ___ + ___ + ___ = ___

5. Which pizza topping did Kira's classmates like the most?

   _____

6. Which pizza topping did Kira's classmates like the least?

   _____

20.3 Favorite Pizza Topping Data Collection

Name: _____ Date: _____

Graphing Paper
Make a graph using clues from the lesson.

Average Rainfall in Tokyo	
January	
February	
March	
April	
May	
June	
July	
August	
September	
October	
November	
December	

● = 2 inches

29   20.4 Problem Solve: Read and Interpret Data

Name: _____ Date: _____

Graphing Paper
Use this data to make a tally chart.

46	50	54	48	53	47	48
49	52	50	53	50	46	51
48	52	46	52	48	51	47
47	49	53	50	46	53	50
54	48	53	50	47	52	54

Height of Second Graders

Inches	Tally Marks
46-48	
49-51	
52-54	

20.5 Compare Measurement Data

Next page

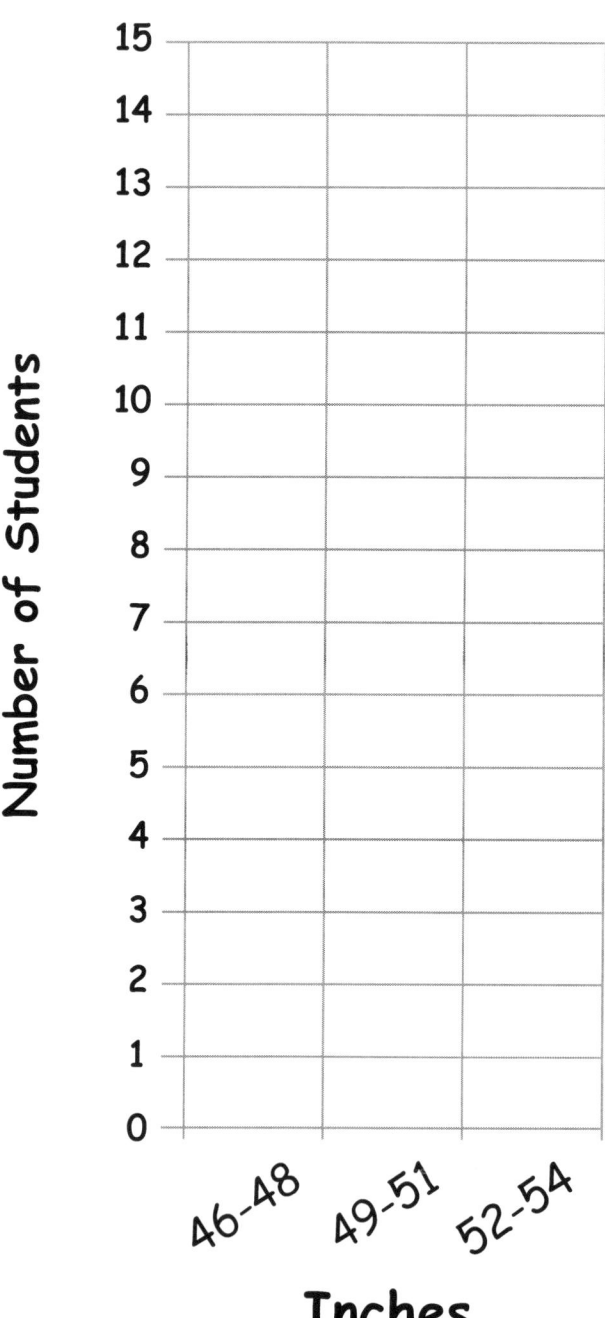

Name: _____ Date: _____

Compare Measurement Data
How tall are these students? Record their heights on the lines below.

_____ inches

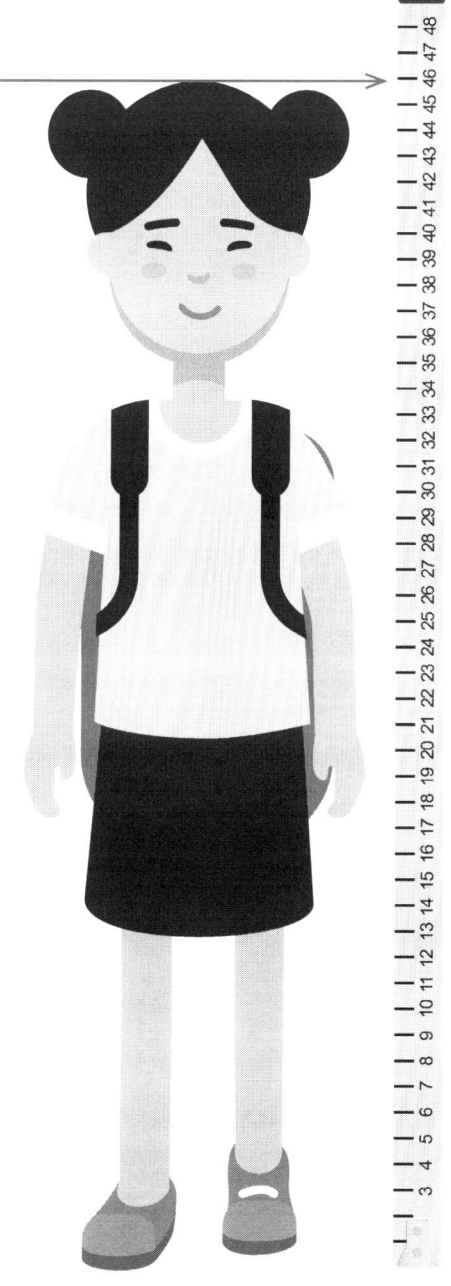

_____ inches

20.5 Compare Measurement Data

_____ inches　　　　　　　　_____ inches

20.5 Compare Measurement Data

_____ inches   _____ inches

20.5 Compare Measurement Data

_____ inches   _____ inches

20.5 Compare Measurement Data

_____ inches

_____ inches

20.5 Compare Measurement Data

36

Next page

Use your measurements to make a tally chart. Then use the data in your tally chart to make a bar graph.

Height of Students	
Inches	Tally Marks
46-48	
49-51	
52-54	
55-57	

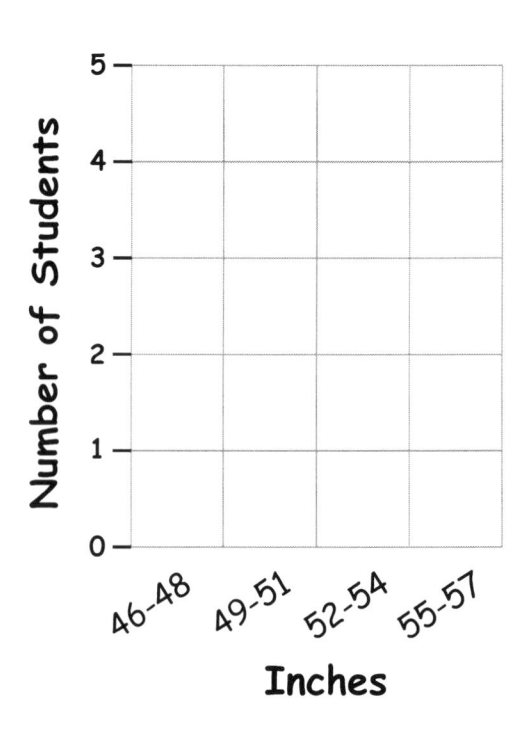

1. How many 2nd graders are 46-48 inches tall?

   ___

2. How many 2nd graders were measured in total?

   ___

3. How many 2nd graders are 52-57 inches tall?

   ___ + ___ = ___

4. How many 2nd graders are 46-51 inches tall?

   ___ + ___ = ___

Name: _____ Date: _____

Thousand Chart

Use the number patterns on this chart to count by 100s!

1000

10	20	30	40	50	60	70	80	90	100
110	120	130	140	150	160	170	180	190	200
210	220	230	240	250	260	270	280	290	300
310	320	330	340	350	360	370	380	390	400
410	420	430	440	450	460	470	480	490	500
510	520	530	540	550	560	570	580	590	600
610	620	630	640	650	660	670	680	690	700
710	720	730	740	750	760	770	780	790	800
810	820	830	840	850	860	870	880	890	900
910	920	930	940	950	960	970	980	990	1000

21.1 Add Hundreds

Name: _____ Date: _____

Add Hundreds

Which addition sentences are true? Color the addition sentences that have the correct sums.

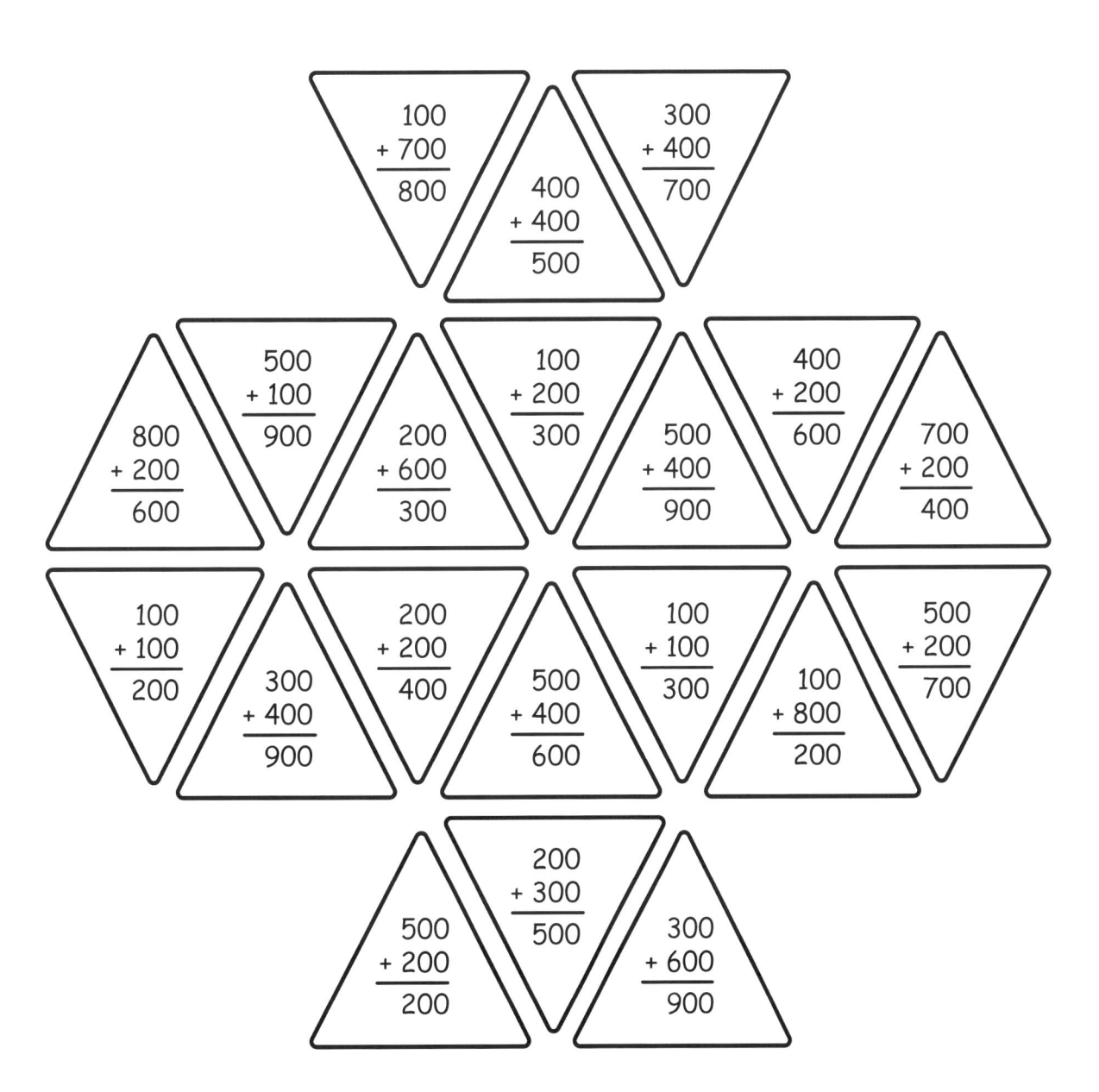

- 100 + 700 = 800
- 400 + 400 = 500
- 300 + 400 = 700
- 800 + 200 = 600
- 500 + 100 = 900
- 200 + 600 = 300
- 100 + 200 = 300
- 500 + 400 = 900
- 400 + 200 = 600
- 700 + 200 = 400
- 100 + 100 = 200
- 300 + 400 = 900
- 200 + 200 = 400
- 500 + 400 = 600
- 100 + 100 = 300
- 100 + 800 = 200
- 500 + 200 = 700
- 500 + 200 = 200
- 200 + 300 = 500
- 300 + 600 = 900

21.1 Add Hundreds   40

Name: _____ Date: _____

Break Apart 3-Digit Numbers to Add (without Regrouping)

Use the place-value charts to find the missing sums.
Then match each sum to a letter to solve the riddle.

What do you call a very small valentine?

A $\overline{\text{v}}$ $\overline{\text{a}}$ $\overline{\text{l}}$ $\overline{\text{e}}$ $\overline{\text{n}}$ $\overline{\text{t}}$ $\overline{\text{i}}$ $\overline{\text{n}}$ $\overline{\text{y}}$
  999 673 457 273 534 983 286 659 387

H	T	O
1	7	1
1	0	2

$\overline{\ }\ \overline{\ }\ \overline{\ }$
e

H	T	O
2	5	2
1	3	5

$\overline{\ }\ \overline{\ }\ \overline{\ }$
y

H	T	O
2	4	4
2	1	3

$\overline{\ }\ \overline{\ }\ \overline{\ }$
l

H	T	O
7	6	2
2	3	7

$\overline{\ }\ \overline{\ }\ \overline{\ }$
v

H	T	O
1	7	2
1	1	4

$\overline{\ }\ \overline{\ }\ \overline{\ }$
i

H	T	O
4	3	6
2	2	3

$\overline{\ }\ \overline{\ }\ \overline{\ }$
n

H	T	O
5	4	1
4	4	2

$\overline{\ }\ \overline{\ }\ \overline{\ }$
t

H	T	O
3	1	0
2	2	4

$\overline{\ }\ \overline{\ }\ \overline{\ }$
n

H	T	O
4	2	3
2	5	0

$\overline{\ }\ \overline{\ }\ \overline{\ }$
a

Name: _____ Date: _____

Break Apart 3-Digit Numbers to Add (with Regrouping)

Find each sum by regrouping. Then, match the sum to a color and use crayons to color the rainbow!

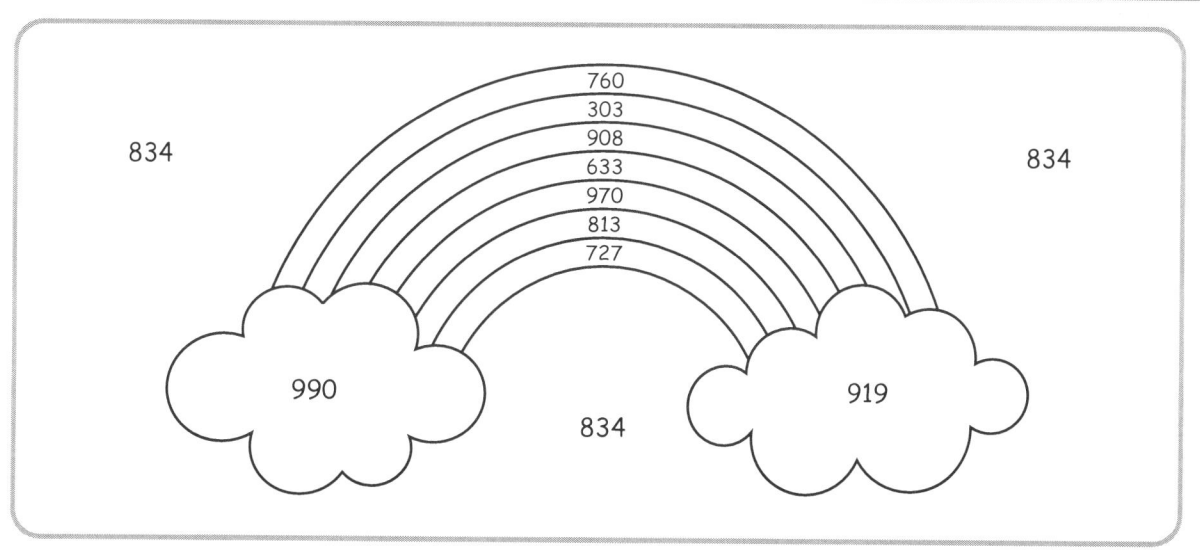

Rainbow colors:
760
303
908
633
970
813
727

834 (left)   834 (right)

990 (left cloud)   919 (right cloud)

834 (bottom)

H	T	O
8	4	2
1	2	8

Light Blue

H	T	O
6	0	6
3	8	4

Gray

H	T	O
5	8	4
1	7	6

Red

H	T	O
3	4	6
2	8	7

Green

H	T	O
6	9	5
1	1	8

Dark Blue

H	T	O
1	9	9
1	0	4

Orange

H	T	O
5	5	7
1	7	0

Purple

H	T	O
7	2	6
1	9	3

Gray

H	T	O
7	1	4
1	9	4

Yellow

H	T	O
4	8	2
3	5	2

Light Blue

21.3 Break Apart 3-Digit Numbers to Add (With Regrouping)

Name: _____ Date: _____

Place-Value Chart

Use this place-value chart to find the sum.

Hundreds	Tens	Ones

43   21.4 Add Three-Digit Numbers

Name: _____ Date: _____

Adding 3-Digit Numbers

Find each sum using these place-value charts. Write the addends in each place-value chart, and then add to find the sum!

745 + 9 = ___   425 + 296 = ___   872 + 88 = ___   324 + 6 = ___

H	T	O

H	T	O

H	T	O

H	T	O

___ ___ ___   ___ ___ ___   ___ ___ ___   ___ ___ ___

Look at this completed place-value chart. Why is there a 1 above the tens place? Use a complete sentence in your answer.

    1

H	T	O
5	2	7
		6

  5 3 3

_____

_____

_____

21.4 Add Three-Digit Numbers

44

Name: _____ Date: _____

Addition Paper

Use the place-value chart below to solve this word problem.

Alice has 566 puzzle pieces. Theo has 357 puzzle pieces. How many puzzle pieces do they have altogether?

Step 1: Circle the Numbers. These are the addends!
Step 2: Underline the Question. What are you solving?
Step 3: Find the Key Words. Do you see *altogether, in total, more, plus,* or *add*?
Step 4: Write the Addition Sentence. ___ + ___ = ___
Step 5: Find the Sum. Solve the addition sentence.

Hundreds	Tens	Ones

21.5 Problem Solving: 3-Digit Addition

Name: _____ Date: _____

Problem Solving: 3-Digit Addition

Follow the steps below to solve each word problem.
Step 1: Circle the Numbers. These are the addends!
Step 2: Underline the Question. What are you solving?
Step 3: Find the Key Words. Do you see altogether, in total, more, plus, or add?
Step 4: Write the Addition Sentence. ___ + ___ = ___
Step 5: Find the Sum. Solve the addition sentence.

Aria has 146 stuffies. Camila has 138 stuffies. How many stuffies do they have altogether?

H	T	O

___ ___ ___

Carlos has 327 blocks. Mario has 289 blocks. How many blocks do they have in total?

H	T	O

___ ___ ___

Amir painted 319 rocks. Dorsa painted 293 rocks. How many rocks did they paint in total?

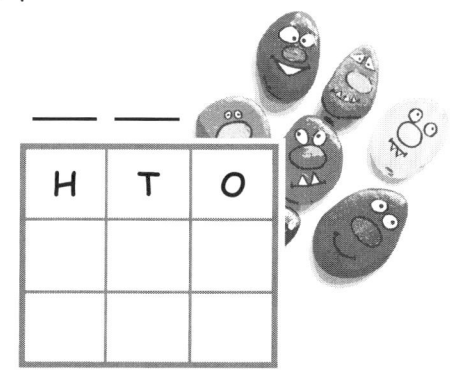

H	T	O

___ ___ ___

Kylie kicked the soccer ball 488 times. Oliana kicked the soccer ball 458 times. How many times did they kick the soccer ball altogether?

H	T	O

___ ___ ___

21.5 Problem Solving: 3-Digit Addition

Practice writing your own word problem using the addends 342 and 209.

_____

_____

_____

_____

_____

Check your work: ✓

Did you use the addends 342 and 209? ☐
Did you write a question? ☐
Did you use a key word like *altogether* or *in total*? ☐

Name: _____ Date: _____

Thousand Chart 1000

10	20	30	40	50	60	70	80	90	100
110	120	130	140	150	160	170	180	190	200
210	220	230	240	250	260	270	280	290	300
310	320	330	340	350	360	370	380	390	400
410	420	430	440	450	460	470	480	490	500
510	520	530	540	550	560	570	580	590	600
610	620	630	640	650	660	670	680	690	700
710	720	730	740	750	760	770	780	790	800
810	820	830	840	850	860	870	880	890	900
910	920	930	940	950	960	970	980	990	1000

1. 500 - 200 = _____

2. 900 - 100 = _____

3. 700 - 300 = _____

22.1 Subtract Hundreds

Name: _____ Date: _____

Subtract Hundreds

Find the difference by subtracting the hundreds and ignoring the zeros. Color the cars when you are done!

700 - 100 =

400 - 300 =

800 - 200 =

300 - 100 =

49

22.1 Subtract Hundreds

Next page

900 - 200 =

500 - 300 =

800 - 400 =

600 - 300 =

900 - 500 =

700 - 600 =

22.1 Subtract Hundreds

Name: _____ Date: _____

Break Apart 3-Digit Numbers to Subtract (Without Regrouping)

Use the place-value charts to find the missing differences. Then draw a line to the correct pair of tires.

H	T	O
8	5	7
2	4	3

___ ___ ___

H	T	O
4	9	2
3	1	1

___ ___ ___

H	T	O
9	3	8
4	2	6

___ ___ ___

H	T	O
5	6	9
2	3	7

___ ___ ___

H	T	O
7	8	3
3	5	3

___ ___ ___

512

614

430

332

181

51 22.2 Break Apart 3-Digit Numbers to Subtract (Without Regrouping)

Name: _____ Date: _____

Subtraction Page

Use this paper to find the difference. You will need a crayon to cross out digits when you regroup.

642 - 254 = _____

Hundreds	Tens	Ones

22.3 Break Apart 3-Digit Numbers to Subtract (With Regrouping)

Break Apart 3-Digit Numbers to Add

Can you find the difference? Do not forget to regroup!

Example:

          8   14

H	T	O
9̸	4̸	5
1	5	0

   7   9   5

H	T	O
4	6	3
2	8	0

___ ___ ___

H	T	O
8	7	7
6	2	9

___ ___ ___

H	T	O
3	3	1
1	1	4

___ ___ ___

H	T	O
3	6	5
1	7	5

___ ___ ___

H	T	O
6	3	2
4	5	5

___ ___ ___

H	T	O
9	5	6
3	8	0

___ ___ ___

H	T	O
7	4	0
5	3	3

___ ___ ___

H	T	O
5	4	6
2	8	3

___ ___ ___

H	T	O
4	0	9
1	8	0

___ ___ ___

H	T	O
7	1	4
2	5	2

___ ___ ___

53   22.3 Break Apart 3-Digit Numbers to Subtract (With Regrouping)

Name: _____ Date: _____

Subtraction Page

Use your pencil and crayons to subtract these numbers on the place-value chart.

305 - 27 = _____

Hundreds	Tens	Ones

22.4 Subtract 3-Digit Numbers

Name: _____ Date: _____

Subtract 3-Digit Numbers

Can you find the differences? Do not forget to regroup! Color the car by looking at which differences match which colors.

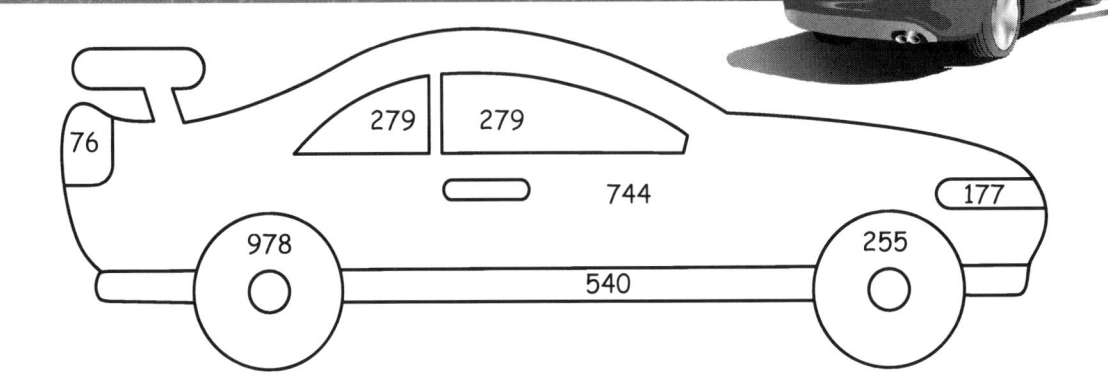

Car image with regions labeled: 76, 279, 279, 744, 177, 978, 540, 255

H	T	O
7	5	2
		8

H	T	O
3	0	4
	2	5

H	T	O
4	2	5
3	4	9

H	T	O
1	8	4
		7

H	T	O
8	9	7
3	5	7

H	T	O
9	9	4
	1	6

H	T	O
2	6	3
		8

H	T	O
5	2	0
	1	4

Color Key: Yellow 177 • Gray 540 • Black 255 • Blue 279 • Green 744 • Purple 506 • Red 76 • Black 978

55

22.4 Subtract 3-Digit Numbers

Name: _____ Date: _____

Subtraction Page

Use your pencil and crayons to subtract these numbers on the place-value chart.

Adrian brought 442 candies to the racetrack. He and his friends ate 182 candies while watching the race cars. How many candies does Adrian have left?

Step 1: Circle the Numbers. This is the whole and the part!
Step 2: Underline the Question. What are you solving?
Step 3: Find the Key Words. Do you see *difference, remain, than, fewer, take away, left, less?* Draw a rectangle.
Step 4: Write the Subtraction Sentence. ___ - ___ = ___
Step 5: Find the Difference. Solve the subtraction sentence.

Hundreds	Tens	Ones

22.5 Problem Solving: 3-Digit Subtraction

Name: _____ Date: _____

Problem Solving: 3-Digit Subtraction

Follow the steps below to solve each word problem.
Step 1: Circle the Numbers. This is the whole and the part!
Step 2: Underline the Question. What are you solving?
Step 3: Find the Key Words. Do you see *difference, remain, than, fewer, take away, left,* or *less*? Draw a rectangle.
Step 4: Write the Subtraction Sentence. ___ - ___ = ___
Step 5: Find the Difference. Solve the subtraction sentence.

---

512 sprint cars raced in the morning, and 349 stock cars raced in the evening. How many more sprint cars raced than stock cars?

H	T	O

Ramona has 643 race car toys. She let her friends borrow 155 of them. How many race car toys does Ramona have left?

H	T	O

James painted 781 yellow and blue race cars. If 267 race cars are yellow, how many blue cars remain?

H	T	O

The pit crew filled a race car with fuel in 433 seconds. Then they filled the race car with fuel in 293 seconds. What is the difference between these times?

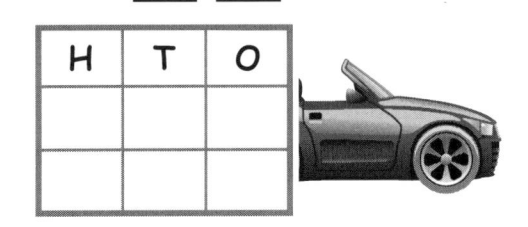

H	T	O

57   22.5 Problem Solving: 3-Digit Subtraction

Next page

Can you write your own subtraction word problem? Use 868 as the whole and 522 as the part. Do not forget the question and key word!

_____

_____

_____

_____

_____

Check your work: ✓

Did you use 868 as the whole and 522 as the part? ☐
Did you write a question? ☐
Did you use a key word like *difference* or *than*? ☐

22.5 Problem Solving: 3-Digit Subtraction

Name: _____ Date: _____

Game Board
Can you add and subtract?

1. Hook your paper clip onto your pencil and use it as a spinner.
   What number did you land on?

   ___

2. Spin again!

   What number did you land on?

   ___

3. Add your numbers together.

   ```
     __
   + __
   ====
     __
   ```

4. Subtract your numbers. Use the larger number as the whole.

   ```
     __
   - __
   ====
     __
   ```

Spinner: 12 | 23 | 34 | 45

59

23.1 Add and Subtract Numbers up to 100

Name: _____   Date: _____

Add and Subtract Numbers up to 100

Can you add and subtract to find these sums and differences?

```
  53
+ 17
```

```
  32
+ 26
```

```
  59
+ 39
```

```
  46
+ 23
```

```
  74
+ 17
```

```
  85
- 72
```

```
  52
- 29
```

```
  46
- 42
```

```
  90
- 35
```

```
  33
- 17
```

23.1 Add and Subtract Numbers up to 100

Name: _____ Date: _____

Practice Page

Can you add 745 + 239?

Can you subtract 907 - 453?

61   23.2 Add and Subtract Numbers up to 1000

Name: _____ Date: _____

What Operation?

What is the missing operation? Complete each number sentence using a plus sign (+) or a minus sign (-).

Example:

56 _−_ 13 = 43

```
  56          56
+ 13        − 13
  ──          ──
  69          43
```

44 ___ 40 = 4

```
  44          44
+ 40        − 40
  ──          ──
```

33 ___ 17 = 50

```
  33          33
+ 17        − 17
  ──          ──
```

62 ___ 35 = 27

```
  62          62
+ 35        − 35
  ──          ──
```

69 ___ 25 = 44

```
  69          69
+ 25        − 25
  ──          ──
```

23.3 What Operation?

59 ___ 32 = 91

$$\begin{array}{r} 59 \\ + 32 \\ \hline \end{array}$$

$$\begin{array}{r} 59 \\ - 32 \\ \hline \end{array}$$

35 ___ 23 = 58

$$\begin{array}{r} 35 \\ + 23 \\ \hline \end{array}$$

$$\begin{array}{r} 35 \\ - 23 \\ \hline \end{array}$$

46 ___ 41 = 87

$$\begin{array}{r} 46 \\ + 41 \\ \hline \end{array}$$

$$\begin{array}{r} 46 \\ - 41 \\ \hline \end{array}$$

71 ___ 21 = 50

$$\begin{array}{r} 71 \\ + 21 \\ \hline \end{array}$$

$$\begin{array}{r} 71 \\ - 21 \\ \hline \end{array}$$

67 ___ 24 = 43

$$\begin{array}{r} 67 \\ + 24 \\ \hline \end{array}$$

$$\begin{array}{r} 67 \\ - 24 \\ \hline \end{array}$$

19 ___ 16 = 35

$$\begin{array}{r} 19 \\ + 16 \\ \hline \end{array}$$

$$\begin{array}{r} 19 \\ - 16 \\ \hline \end{array}$$

Name: _____ Date: _____

Ways to Make a Number

Make each number below. Use two of the numbers in the circles to add or subtract. When you find the correct answer, color in the two circles that you used!

Example:

27

(37) (17) (4) (10)

$$\begin{array}{r} 17 \\ +\ 10 \\ \hline 27 \end{array}$$

43

(19) (24) (74) (11)

$$\begin{array}{r} \_\_ \\ +\ \_\_ \\ \hline \_\_ \end{array}$$

6

(52) (3) (38) (46)

$$\begin{array}{r} \_\_ \\ -\ \_\_ \\ \hline \_\_ \end{array}$$

67

(10) (26) (41) (9)

$$\begin{array}{r} \_\_ \\ +\ \_\_ \\ \hline \_\_ \end{array}$$

35

(87) (32) (90) (55)

$$\begin{array}{r} \_\_ \\ -\ \_\_ \\ \hline \_\_ \end{array}$$

23.4 Ways to Make a Number

Next page

91
(98) (32) (2) (59)

$$+\frac{\overline{}}{\overline{}}$$

23
(61) (84) (77) (23)

$$-\frac{\overline{}}{\overline{}}$$

89
(27) (18) (45) (62)

$$+\frac{\overline{}}{\overline{}}$$

38
(29) (14) (65) (27)

$$-\frac{\overline{}}{\overline{}}$$

60
(29) (22) (38) (33)

$$+\frac{\overline{}}{\overline{}}$$

61
(12) (96) (73) (42)

$$-\frac{\overline{}}{\overline{}}$$

23.4 Ways to Make a Number

Name: _____ Date: _____

Hundred Chart
Use this hundred chart to find the number.

100

1	2	3	4	5	6	7	8	9	10
11	12	13	14	15	16	17	18	19	20
21	22	23	24	25	26	27	28	29	30
31	32	33	34	35	36	37	38	39	40
41	42	43	44	45	46	47	48	49	50
51	52	53	54	55	56	57	58	59	60
61	62	63	64	65	66	67	68	69	70
71	72	73	74	75	76	77	78	79	80
81	82	83	84	85	86	87	88	89	90
91	92	93	94	95	96	97	98	99	100

23.5 What's My Number?

What's My Number?

Find each number based on the clues below.

Clues	What's the Number?
Example: 1. I have 1 digit. 2. I am an odd number. 3. If you add 2 to me, you will get 7. 4. What am I?	5
1. I have 2 digits. 2. I am less than 15 but more than 11. 3. If you subtract 2 from me, you will get 10. 4. What am I?	
1. I have 2 digits. 2. I am less than 20. 3. One of my digits is an 8. 4. What am I?	
1. I have 1 digit. 2. I am an odd number. 3. If you add 4 to me, you will get 7. 4. What am I?	
1. I have 2 digits. 2. I am an even number. 3. I am more than 45 but less than 47. 4. What am I?	
1. I have 1 digit. 2. I am more than 6. 3. If you add 11 to me, you will get 19. 4. What am I?	

Name: _____ Date: _____

Equation Paper

Solve the word problem using this worksheet.

Step 1: What are the numbers?

_____ and _____

Step 2: What is the question? Remember to use a complete sentence.

_____

Step 3: What is the key word?

_____

Step 1: What is the equation?

24.1 Problem-Solving Strategy: Write a Number Sentence

Name: _____ Date: _____

Problem Solving Strategy: Write a Number Sentence

Read each word problem below, and find the answer by writing the equation. Remember to follow these steps:

Step 1: What are the numbers?
Step 2: What is the question?
Step 3: What is the key word?
Step 4: What is the equation?

Walter ran 44 minutes on Saturday and 25 minutes on Sunday. How many minutes did he run altogether?

Jamie swam 31 meters, and her friend swam 63 meters. How many meters did Jamie and her friend swim in total?

Ashley caught 14 fly balls in May. She caught 36 fly balls in June. How many more fly balls did she catch in June than in May?

24.1 Problem-Solving Strategy: Write a Number Sentence

Xavier made 23 baskets in his game on Saturday. He made another 19 baskets in his game on Sunday. How many baskets did he make in all?

Clara threw a baseball 22 miles per hour. Then she threw a softball 9 miles per hour. How much faster did she throw the baseball than the softball?

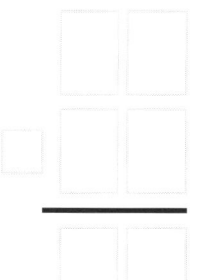

24.1 Problem-Solving Strategy: Write a Number Sentence

Name: _____ Date: _____

Input/Output Table

Can you complete this input/output table? Follow along in the lesson to check your work.

Input	Output
257	
419	
684	
825	

Rule: +135

```
  257        419        684        825
+ 135      + 135      + 135      + 135
-----      -----      -----      -----
```

24.2 Input/Output Boxes: Add

Name: _____ Date: _____

Input/Output Tables: Add

Write addition equations and solve to find the missing output numbers.

Example:

Input	Output
416	764
428	776
435	783
449	797

Rule: +348

```
   1
  416
+ 348
─────
  764
```

```
   1
  428
+ 348
─────
  776
```

```
   1
  435
+ 348
─────
  783
```

```
   1
  449
+ 348
─────
  797
```

Input	Output
329	
358	
415	
487	

Rule: +294

+ _____

+ _____

+ _____

+ _____

24.2 Input/Output Boxes: Add

72

Next page

Input	Output
563	
697	
734	
886	

Rule: +102

Input	Output
109	
214	
275	
327	

Rule: +231

Input	Output
613	
638	
655	
679	

Rule: +228

24.2 Input/Output Boxes: Add

Name: _____ Date: _____

Input/Output Table

What are the missing numbers in the output column? Check your work by following along in the lesson.

Input	Output
560	
678	
754	
880	

Rule: -412

```
  560        678        754        880
- 412      - 412      - 412      - 412
-----      -----      -----      -----
```

24.3 Input/Output Boxes: Subtract

Name: _____ Date: _____

Input/Output Tables: Subtract

Find the missing numbers in each output column by solving the subtraction equations below.

Example:

Input	Output
299	182
346	229
467	350
505	388

Rule: -117

```
   299
 - 117
 -----
   182
```

```
    3 16
   3 4̸ 6̸
 - 117
 -----
   229
```

```
   467
 - 117
 -----
   350
```

```
      9 15
    4 1̸0̸
    5̸ 0̸ 5̸
 - 117
 -----
   388
```

Input	Output
677	
785	
892	
953	

Rule: -202

```
   677
 - 202
 -----
```

```
   785
 - 202
 -----
```

```
   892
 - 202
 -----
```

```
   953
 - 202
 -----
```

24.3 Input/Output Boxes: Subtract

Next page

Input	Output
750	
765	
780	
795	

Rule: -430

```
  750        765
- 430      - 430
-----      -----


  780        795
- 430      - 430
-----      -----
```

Input	Output
890	
943	
975	
998	

Rule: -275

```
  890        943
- 275      - 275
-----      -----


  975        998
- 275      - 275
-----      -----
```

24.3 Input/Output Boxes: Subtract

Input	Output
452	
498	
521	
547	

Rule: -337

```
  452        498
- 337      - 337
-----      -----

  521        547
- 337      - 337
-----      -----
```

Input	Output
676	
698	
736	
790	

Rule: -514

```
  676        698
- 514      - 514
-----      -----

  736        790
- 514      - 514
-----      -----
```

24.3 Input/Output Boxes: Subtract

Name: _____ Date: _____

Word Problem

Practice solving this word problem by following along in the lesson.
Step 1: Circle the Numbers
Step 2: Underline the Question
Step 3: Find the Key Words
Step 4: Write the Equation
Step 5: Draw the Picture

Word Problem:

Rosa is at baseball practice She has hit 635 fly balls and 247 base hits. How many times has Rosa hit the baseball in total?

Write the Equation:

_____

Draw the Picture:

24.4 Problem Solve Using Pictures

Name: _____ Date: _____

Problem Solve Using Pictures

Follow the steps below to solve each word problem.

Step 1: Circle the Numbers.
Step 2: Underline the Question.
Step 3: Find the Key Words.
Step 4: Write the Equation.
Step 5: Draw the Picture

1

Word Problem

Madison scored 429 points in her soccer game. If she scored 241 points in the first half, how many did she score in the second half?

Equation

_____

Picture

2

Word Problem

A dodgeball team threw 709 red balls and 145 orange balls. How many balls did they throw in total?

Equation

_____

Picture

79 24.4 Problem Solve Using Pictures

Word Problem

Jamal danced ballet for 340 minutes and danced tap for 198 minutes. How many minutes did he dance altogether?

Equation

———

Picture

Word Problem

Alice wants to do 512 cartwheels on the balance beam. She has already done 310. How many cartwheels does she have left?

Equation

———

Picture

Word Problem

5 Sophie is working on her ice skating jumps. She has jumped 274 times, but she wants to jump 399 times. How many more jumps does she need to do?

Equation

_____

Picture

Name: _____ Date: _____

Write Word Problems
Use the information below to write your own word problems.

Example:
Equation: 25 + 20 = 45
Topic: Alex is scoring goals in soccer.

Write your word problem here:
_____

Word Problem Checklist:

Did you include the numbers? ☑
Did you write a story? ☑
Did you write a question? ☑
Did you include a key word? ☑

Alex scored 25 goals in his first soccer game. He scored 20 goals in his second game. How many goals did he score altogether?

_____

_____

Equation: 58 - 37 = 21
Topic: Tanya is running laps on the track.

Write your word problem here:
_____

Word Problem Checklist:

Did you include the numbers? ☐
Did you write a story? ☐
Did you write a question? ☐
Did you include a key word? ☐

_____

_____

_____

24.5 Write Word Problems

2

Equation: 44 + 29 = 73
Topic: Yuriy is counting the baseballs he hits during practice.

Write your word problem here:

_____

_____

_____

_____

Word Problem Checklist:

Did you include the numbers? ☐
Did you write a story? ☐
Did you write a question? ☐
Did you include a key word? ☐

3

Equation: 71 + 16 = 87
Topic: Two basketball teams are playing basketball.

Write your word problem here:

_____

_____

_____

_____

Word Problem Checklist:

Did you include the numbers? ☐
Did you write a story? ☐
Did you write a question? ☐
Did you include a key word? ☐

24.5 Write Word Problems

Name: _____ Date: _____

Shapes and Their Attributes

Draw a line between each object and the word that names its shape.

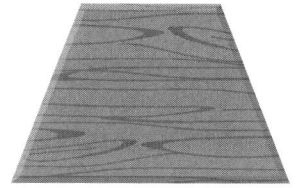

- Circle
- Pentagon 
- Trapezoid 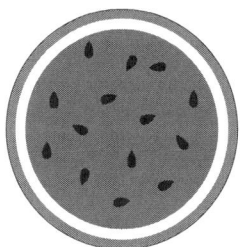
- Square 
- Triangle 

25.1 Two-Dimensional Shapes

Complete the sentences below by choosing words from the word bank.

quadrilaterals	parallel lines	rectangle
hexagon	square	triangle

1. A _____ has 6 sides.

2. A _____ has 4 sides and 2 sets of parallel lines.

3. _____ are lines that are the same distance apart and never meet.

4. A _____ has 4 equal sides and 2 sets of parallel lines.

5. _____ are shapes that have 4 sides.

85   25.1 Two-Dimensional Shapes

Name: _____ Date: _____

Identifying Shapes by Their Angles and Vertices

What shape is being described? Draw a picture of the shape. Draw a picture of the shape in the box.

1. I have 3 sides, 3 angles, and 3 vertices. What shape am I?

   _____

2. I have 4 equal sides, 4 angles, and 4 vertices. What shape am I?

   _____

3. I am perfectly round and have no sides or angles. What shape am I?

   _____

Count and write the number of sides, angles, and vertices (corners) for each shape.

sides: ___
angles: ___
vertices: ___

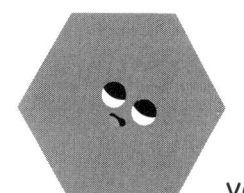

sides: ___
angles: ___
vertices: ___

25.2 Sides and Angles

86

Name: _____ Date: _____

Three-Dimensional Shapes

Draw a line between each object and the word that names its shape.

- rectangular prism
- cylinder
- cube
- sphere
- triangular prism
- cone

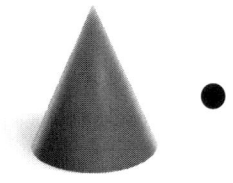

25.3 Three-Dimensional Shapes

Name: _____   Date: _____

Faces, Edges, and Vertices
Circle the shape being described in each section.

1. I have 5 faces, 9 edges, and 6 vertices. What shape am I?

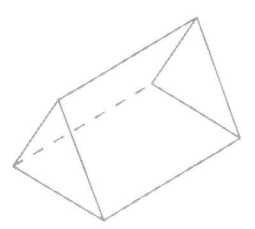

   triangular prism 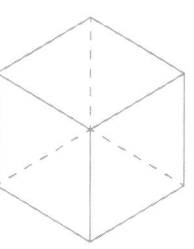   cube

2. I have 2 faces, 0 edges, and 0 vertices. What shape am I?

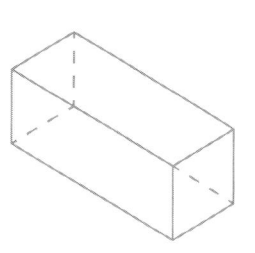

   rectangular prism 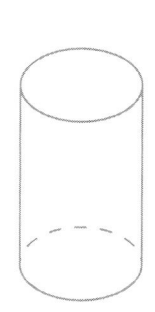   cylinder

3. I have 0 faces, 0 edges, and 0 vertices. What shape am I?

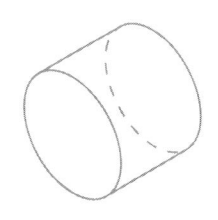

   cylinder 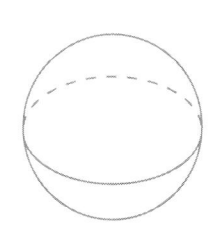   sphere

4. I have 6 faces, 12 edges, and 8 vertices. What shape am I?

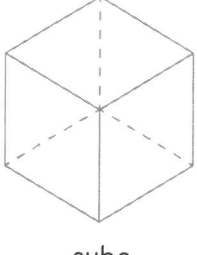

   cube 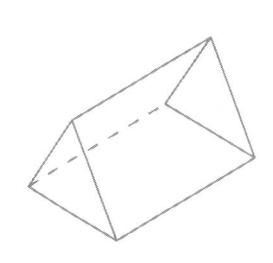   triangular prism

25.4 Faces, Edges, and Vertices

Next page

Shape	Number of faces	Number of edges	Number of vertices

25.4 Faces, Edges, and Vertices

Name: _____ Date: _____

Relate Shapes and Solids

Shapes have different faces. (For example, a triangular prism is made of both triangles and rectangles.) Outline all the squares in blue, all the triangles in red, all the circles in green, and all the rectangles in orange.

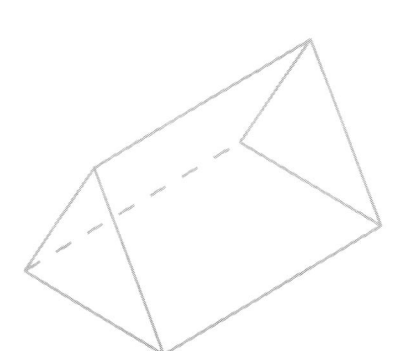

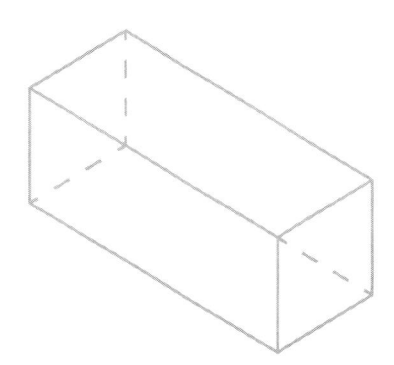

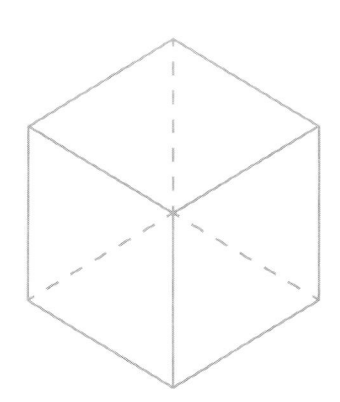

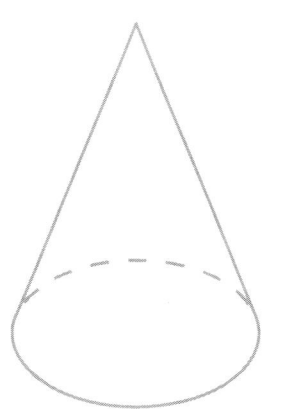

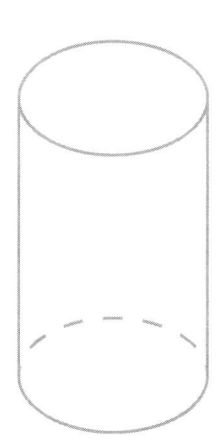

25.5 Relate Shapes and Solids

Name: _____ Date: _____

Wholes

Color **all** parts of each shape the same color to make one whole. Use a different color for each shape.

1.

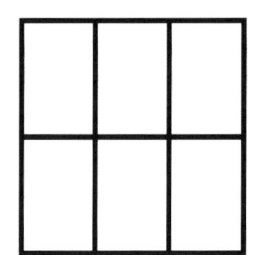

2.

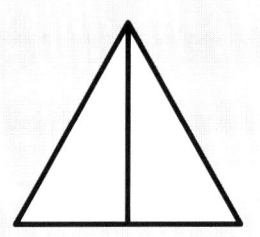

3.

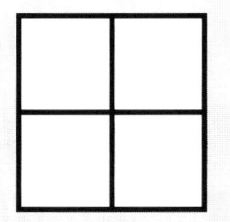

4.

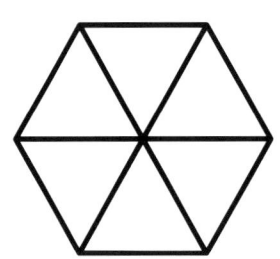

5.

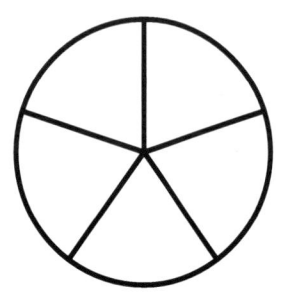

6.

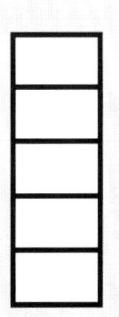

91

26.1 Whole

Name: _____ Date: _____

Halves

Circle the shapes that show 2 halves.

1.

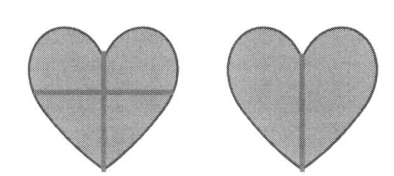

2.

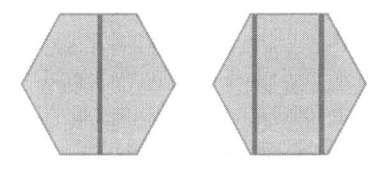

3.

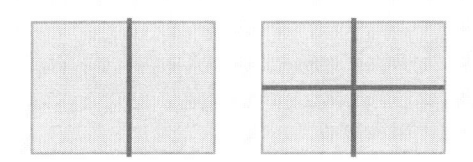

4.

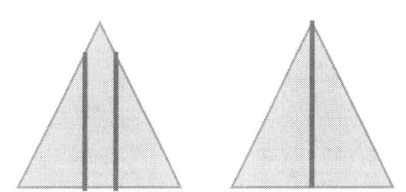

5.

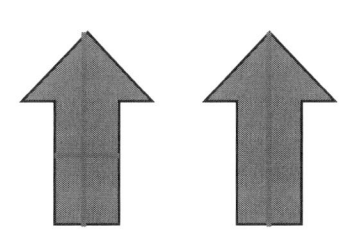

6.

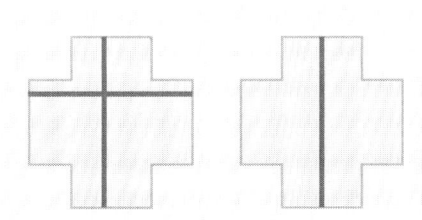

7.

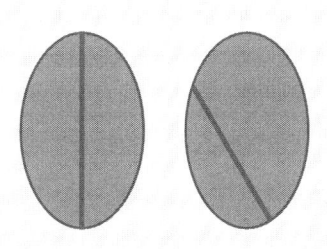

8.

26.2 Halves

92

Next page

Draw a line to divide each shape in half.

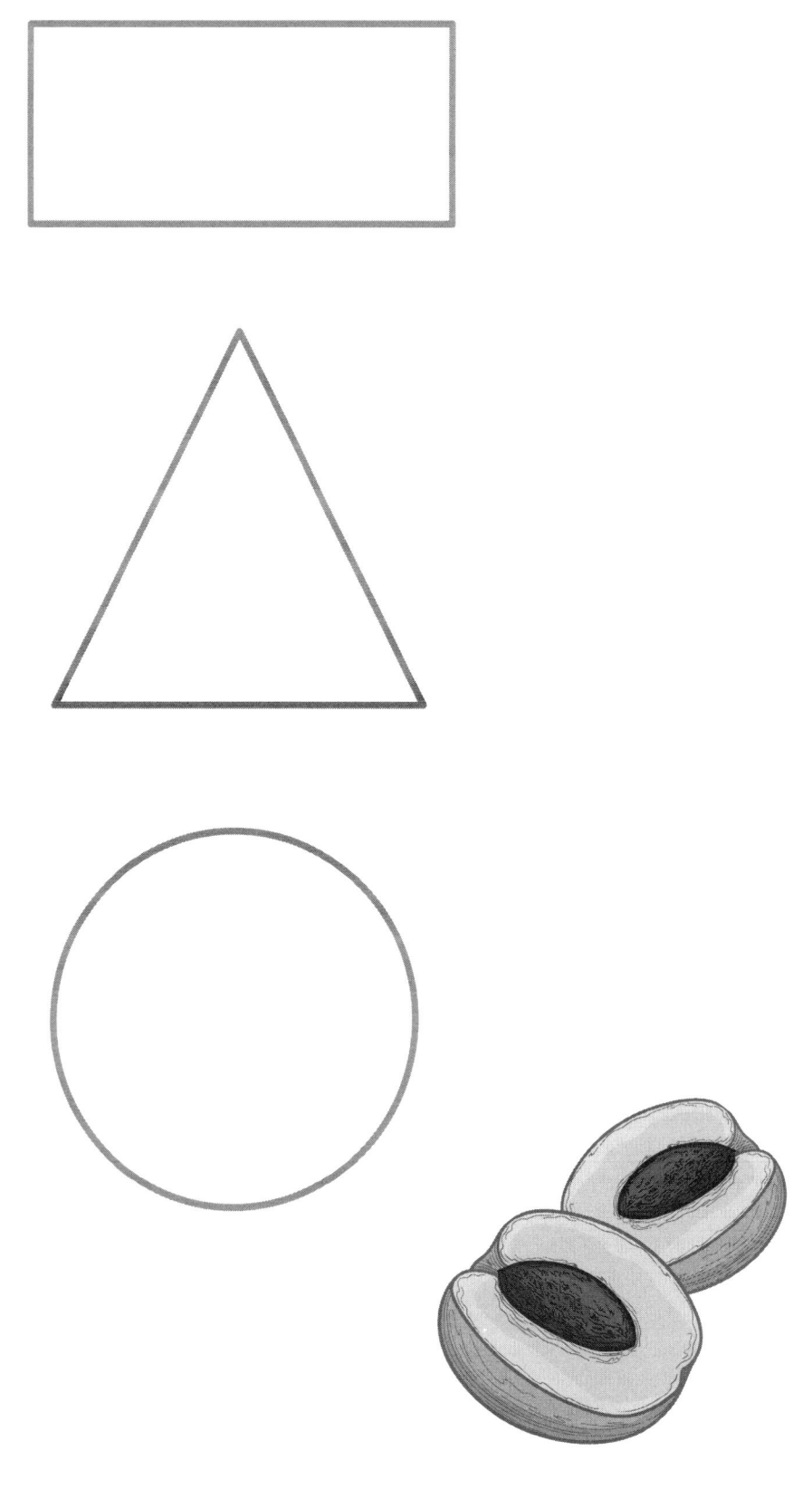

93   26.2 Halves

Name: _____ Date: _____

Thirds
Circle the shape that is divided into thirds.

1.

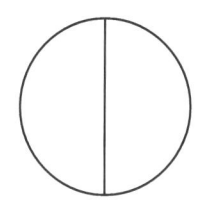

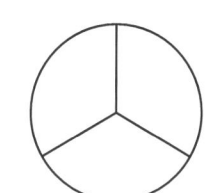

2.

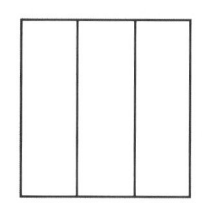

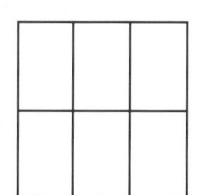

3.

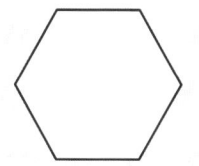

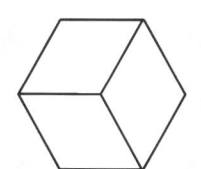

4.

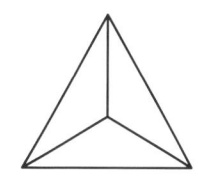

5.

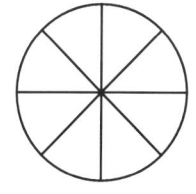

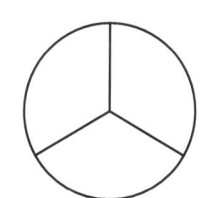

6.

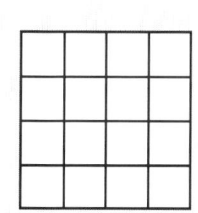

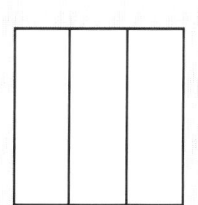

26.3 Thirds

94

Next page

Divide each shape below into thirds (three equal parts).

7.

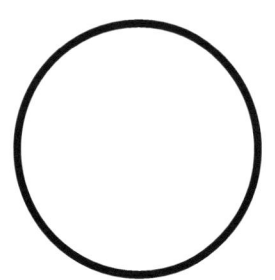

8.

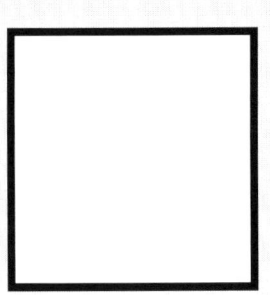

9.

10.

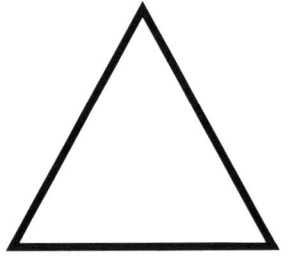

Name: _____ Date: _____

Fourths

Circle the shape that is divided into fourths (4 equal parts).

1.

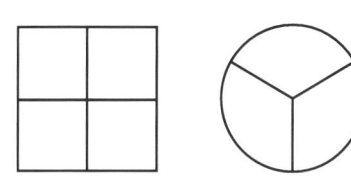

2.

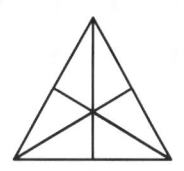

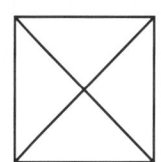

3.

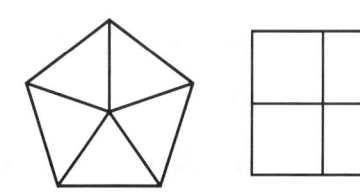

4.

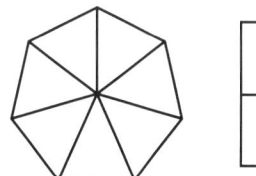

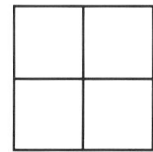

5.

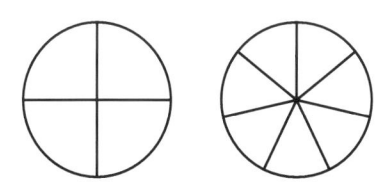

6.

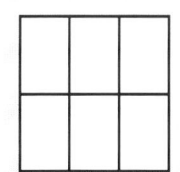

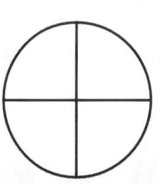

Divide the shapes into fourths by drawing lines two different ways.

7.

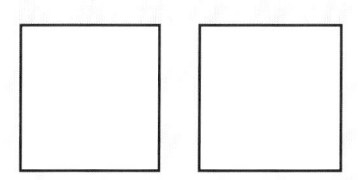

8.

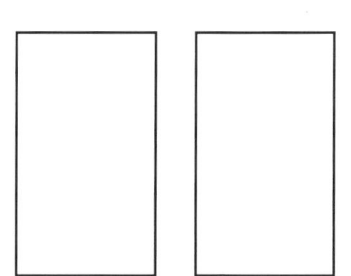

26.4 Fourths

96

Name: _____ Date: _____

Problem Solving: Finding a Pattern
Color in the shape as directed.

1.

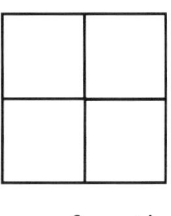

one fourth

2.

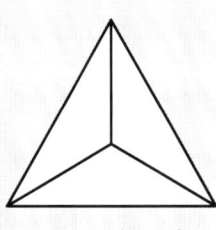

one third

3.

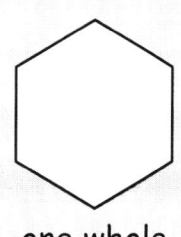

one whole

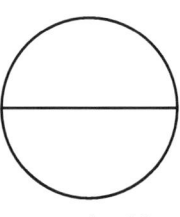

4.

one half

Draw a circle around groups of objects to make halves, thirds, and fourths.

5. Divide the group of arrows into **thirds**.

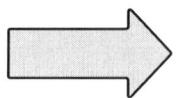

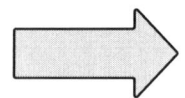

6. Divide the group of stars into **halves**.

7. Divide the group of stars into **fourths**.

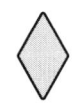

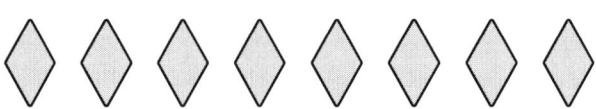

97

26.5 Problem Solving: Find a Pattern

Name: _____ Date: _____

Make Halves

Draw a line to divide each whole shape into two equal parts.

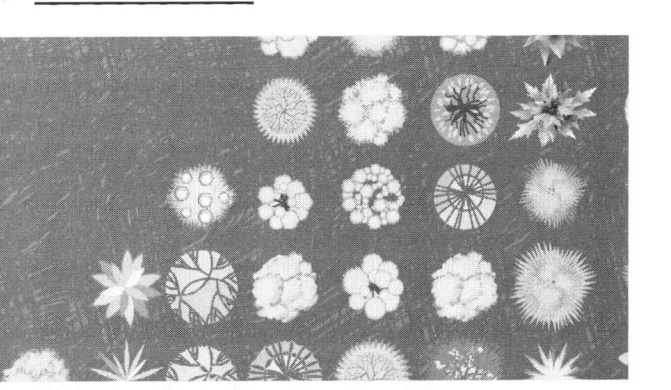

1.

2.

3.

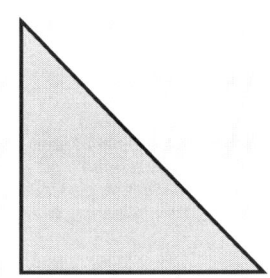

4.

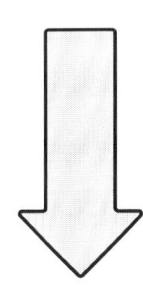

5.

6.

7.

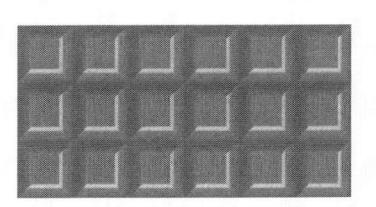

8.

27.1 Make Halves

98

Name: _____ Date: _____

Make Thirds
Draw lines to divide each whole shape into 3 equal parts.

1.

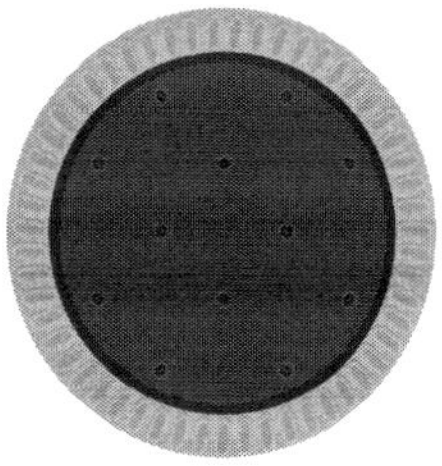

2.

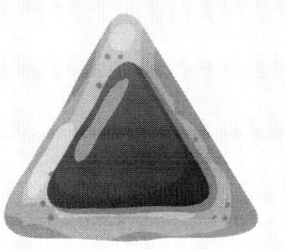

3.

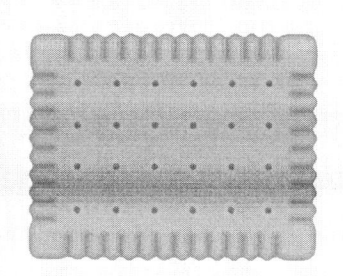

4.

5.

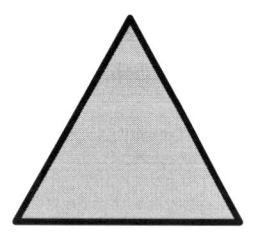

6.

7.

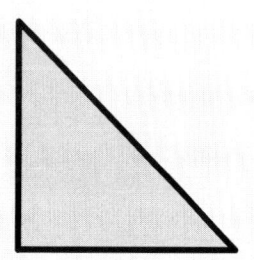

8.

99

27.2 Make Thirds

Name: _____ Date: _____

Make Fourths
Draw a line to divide each whole shape into 4 equal parts.

1.

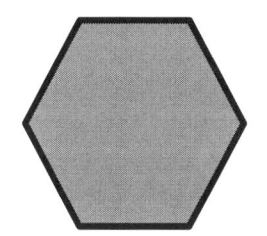

2.

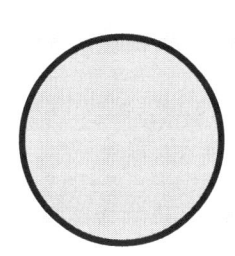

3.

4.

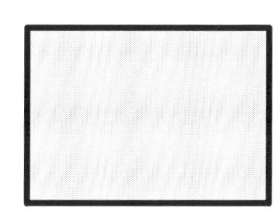

5.

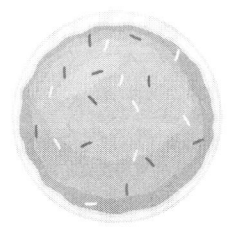

6.

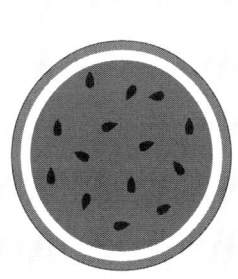

7.

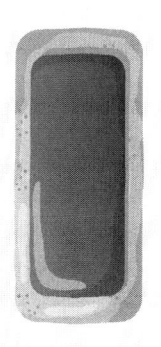

8.

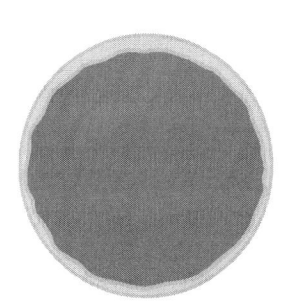

27.3 Make Fourths

100

Name: _____ Date: _____

Partition Shapes

Use crayons to color the shape to make the statement true.

1.

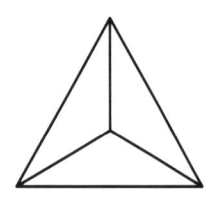

two thirds

2.

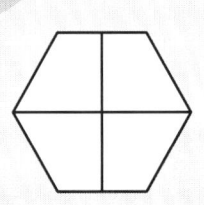

three fourths

3.

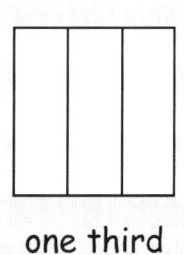

one third

4.

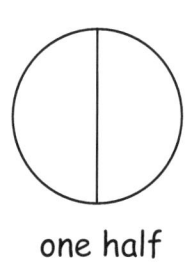

one half

Write the name of the colored part of the shape, for example, two fourths.

5.

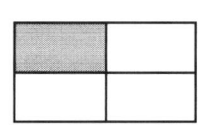

_____

_____

6.

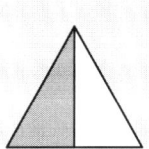

_____

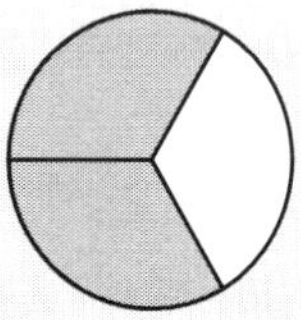

_____

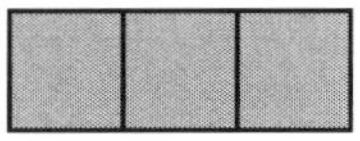

101   27.4 Make a Shape

Name: _____ Date: _____

Equal vs Unequal Parts

Read the directions. Draw a line to divide each shape.

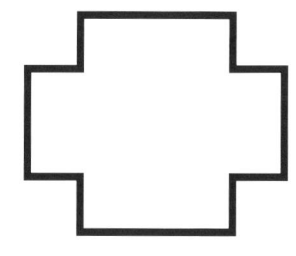

1. Divide the shape into halves.

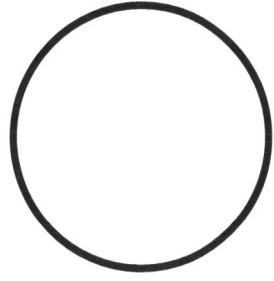

2. Divide the shape into thirds.

3. Divide the shape into fourths.

If the shape is divided equally, write equal on the line. If the shape is divided unequally, write unequal on the line.

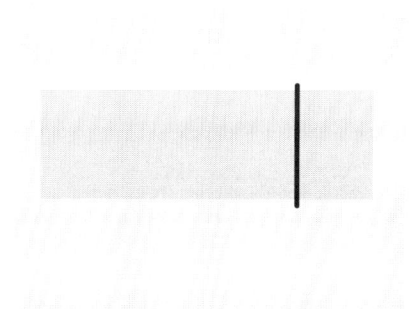

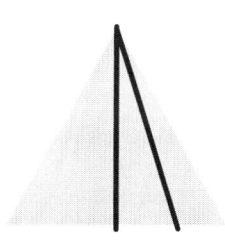

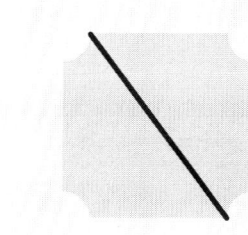

_____   _____   _____

_____   _____   _____

27.5 Equal vs Unequal Parts

102

Name: _____ Date: _____

Pizza Halves

Circle the pizzas that show halves correctly!
Write ½ in each box of each correct pizza.

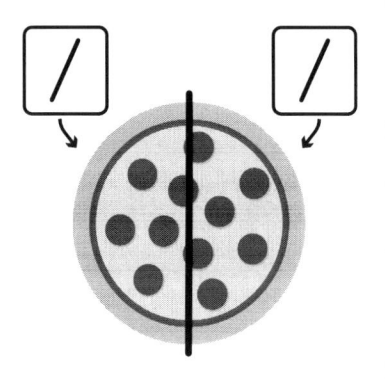

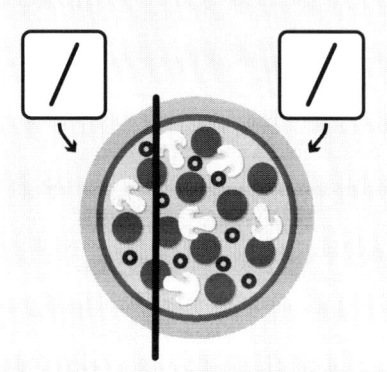

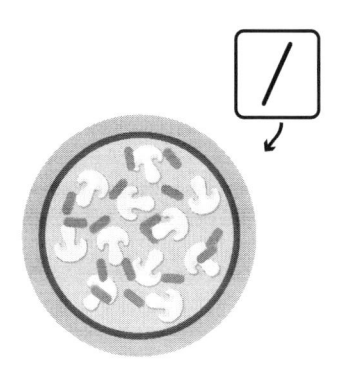

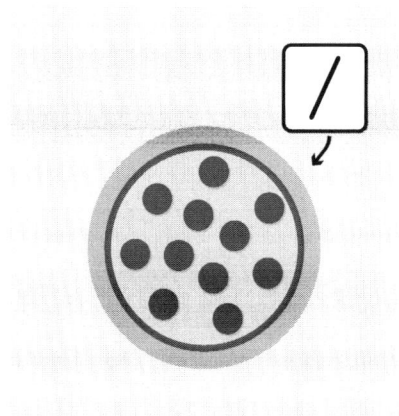

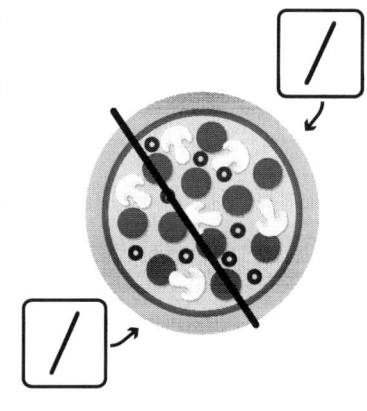

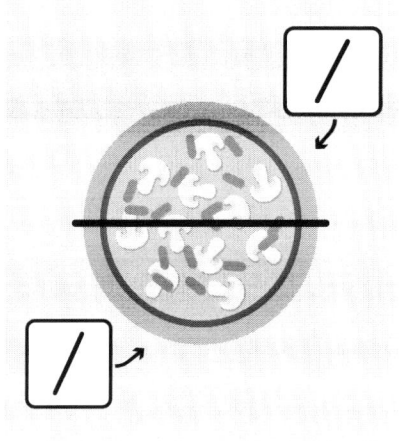

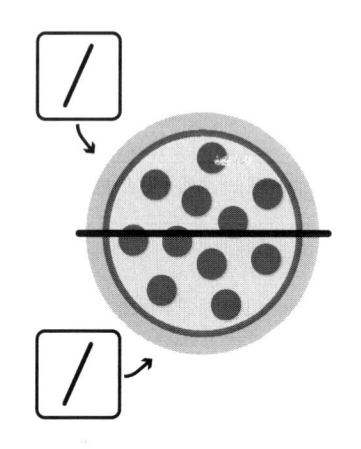

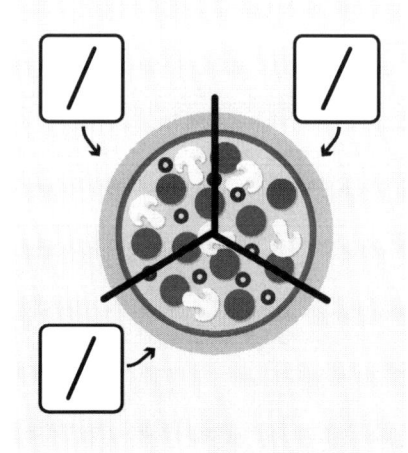

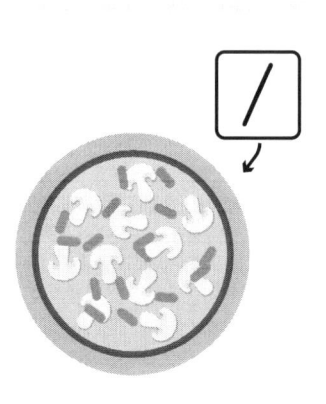

103

28.1 Fractions 1/2

Next page

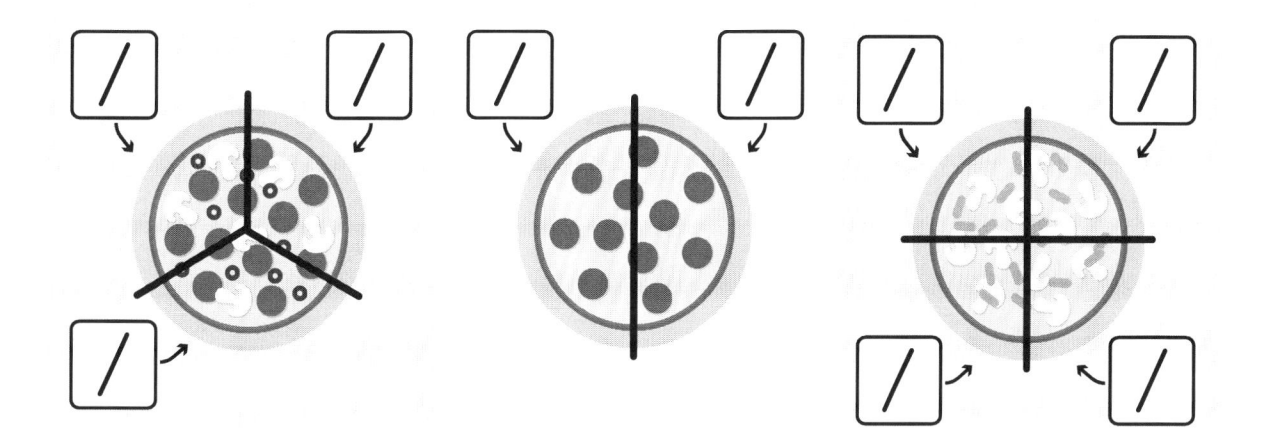

Draw a line from top to bottom to show halves. Color ½ of the pizza brown. Color the other ½ red.

28.1 Fractions 1/2

104

Pizza Thirds

Circle each pizza that shows thirds correctly!
Write 1/3 in each box of the correct pizza.

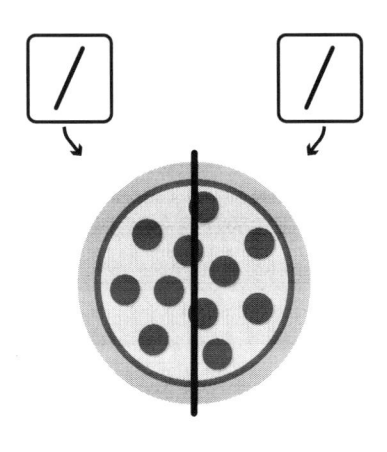

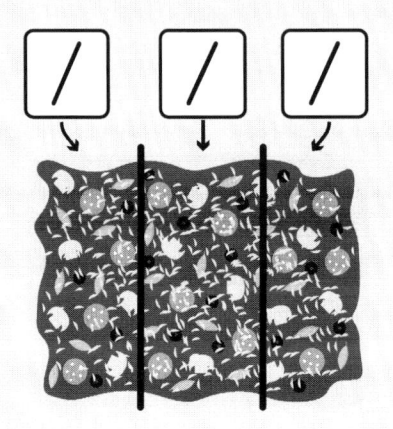

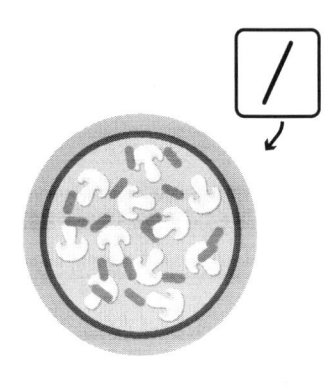

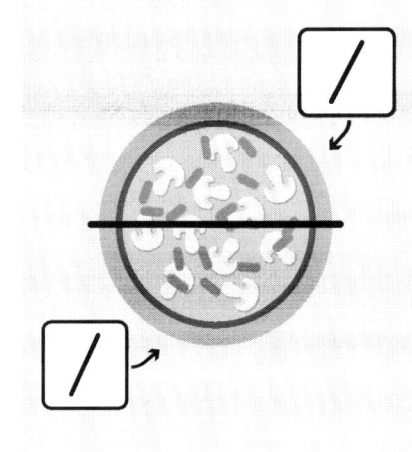

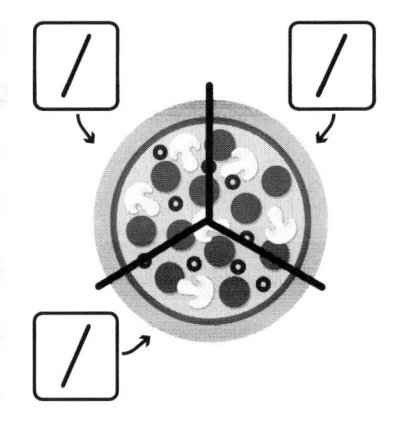

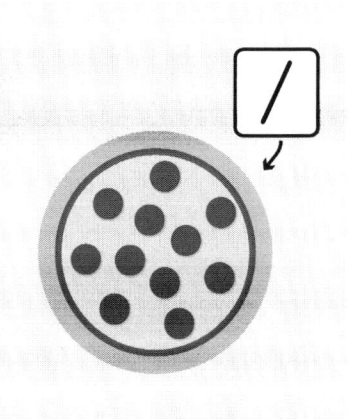

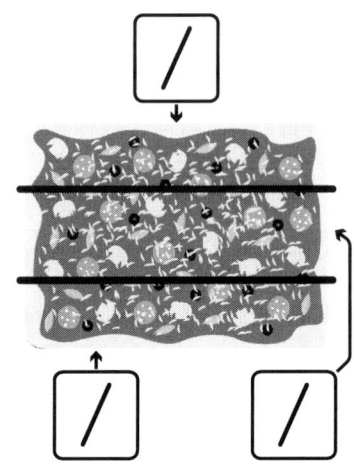

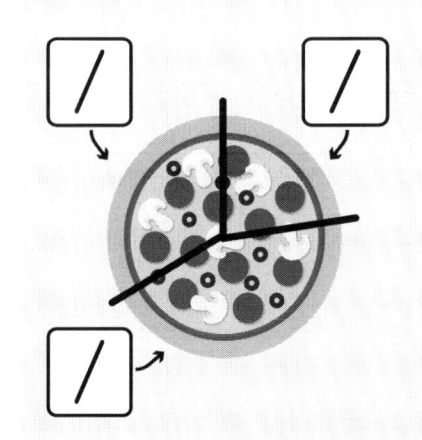

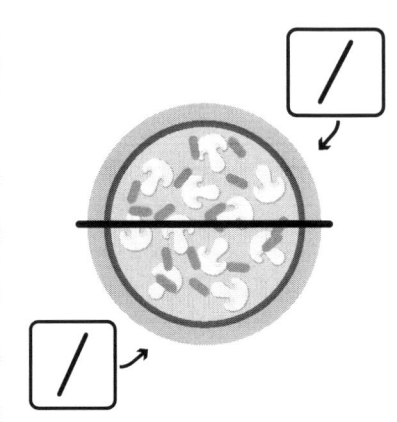

105

28.2 Fractions 1/3

Trace the dotted lines to show the thirds. Color 1/3 of the pizza brown. Color 1/3 of the pizza red. Color 1/3 of the pizza yellow.

Trace the dotted lines to show the thirds. Color 1/3 of the pizza green. Color 1/3 of the pizza orange. Color 1/3 of the pizza red.

Name: _____ Date: _____

Pizza Fourths

Circle the pizzas that show fourths correctly!
Write ¼ in each box of each correct pizza.

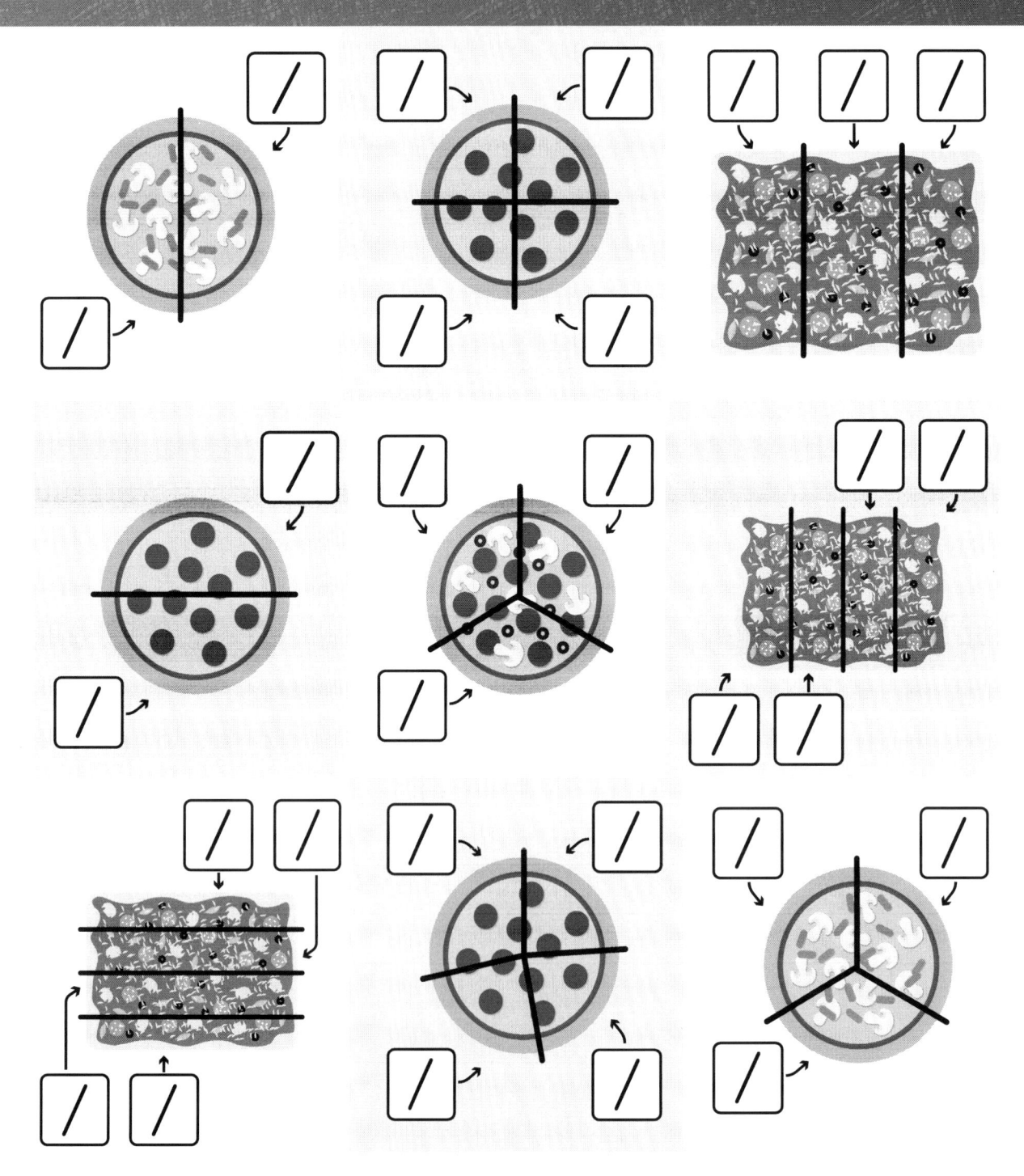

107

28.3 Fractions 1/4

Next pag

Trace the dotted lines to show the fourths. Color ¼ of the pizza brown. Color ¼ of the pizza red. Color ¼ of the pizza yellow. Color ¼ of the pizza green.

Draw 2 or 3 lines to make fourths. Color ¼ of the pizza green. Color ¼ of the pizza orange. Color ¼ of the pizza red. Color ¼ of the pizza yellow.

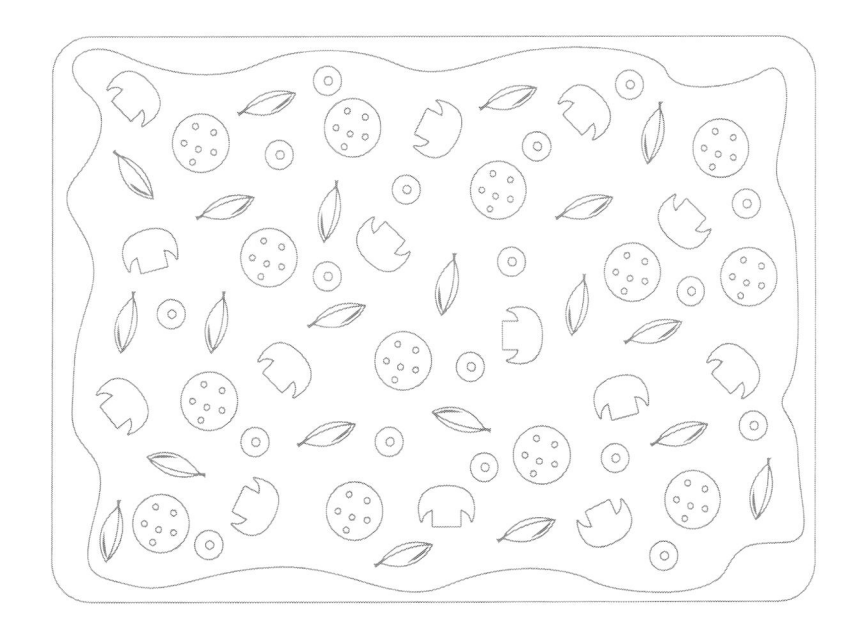

28.3 Fractions 1/4

Name: _____ Date: _____

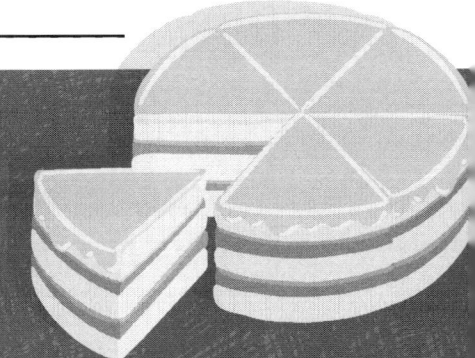

Adding Fractions

Match the parts to make whole shapes!

Example:

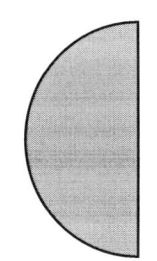

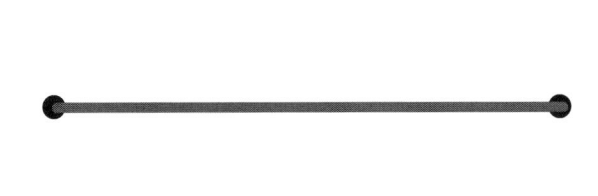

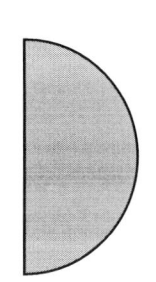

1.

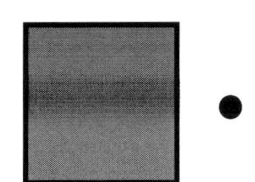

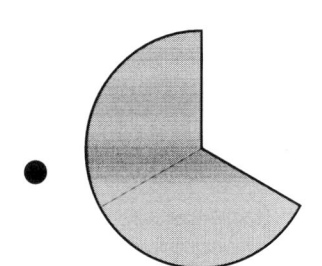

2.

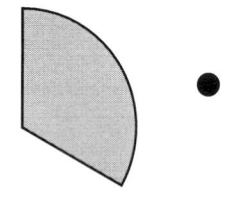

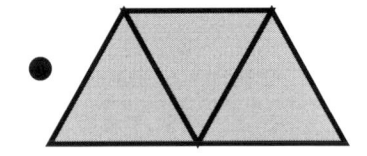

3.

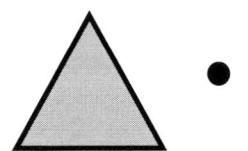

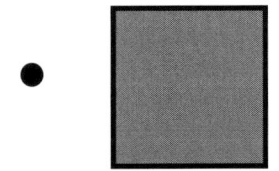

109

28.4 Add Fractions

Next page

Circle the part(s) that make the whole shape. Then draw the whole shape in the box.

4.

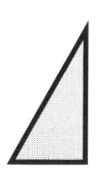

$$\frac{1}{2} + \frac{1}{2} = 1$$

5.

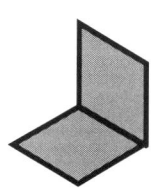

$$\frac{1}{3} + \frac{2}{3} = 1$$

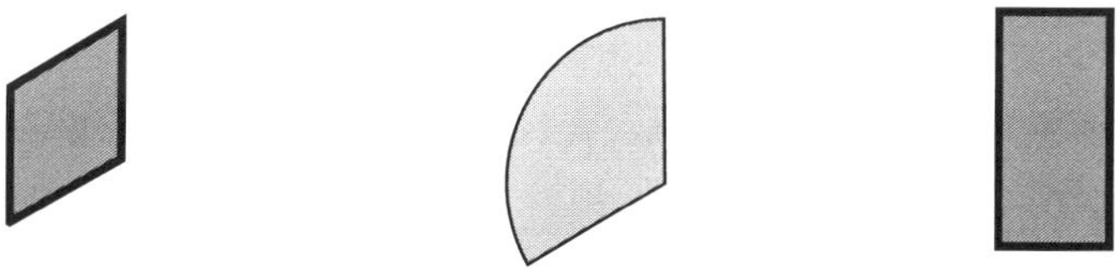

6.

$$\frac{1}{4} + \frac{3}{4} = 1$$

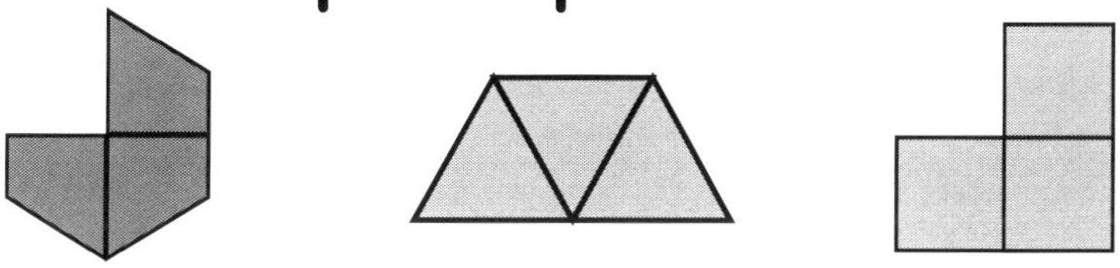

28.4 Add Fractions

Name: _____ Date: _____

Fraction Word Problems

1. Read each problem.
2. Color the parts that are in the problem using the correct color.
3. Color the parts left over with a gray crayon.
4. Circle the answer to the problem that matches your picture!

1. ½ of the circle house is painted yellow. What part of the house is not painted?

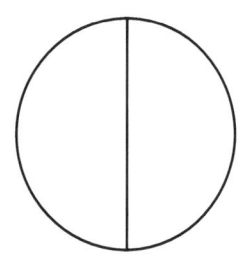

$\frac{1}{3}$ $\frac{1}{2}$ $\frac{1}{4}$

3. ⅓ of the hexagon house is painted green. What part of the house is not painted?

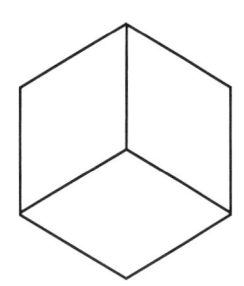

$\frac{1}{2}$ $\frac{3}{4}$ $\frac{2}{3}$

4. ¾ of the triangle house is painted orange. What part of the house is not painted?

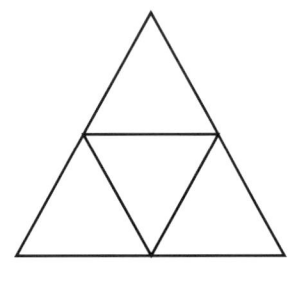

$\frac{1}{4}$ $\frac{3}{4}$ $\frac{1}{3}$

111

28.5 Problem Solving

Name: _____ Date: _____

Word Problem Match

Match the word problem to the correct whole. Then find the fraction and color it using the information from the word problem. Color the rest of the shape gray. Then circle the correct fraction.

Example:

1/2 of the hexagon house is painted pink. What part of the house is not painted? ————— $\frac{1}{3}$ ($\frac{1}{2}$) $\frac{3}{4}$

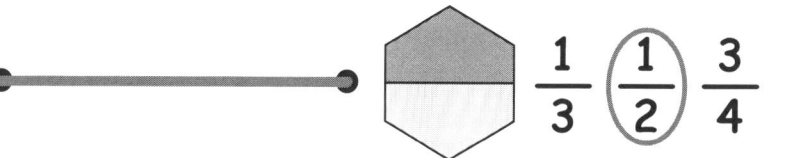

1. 1/2 of the rectangle house is painted red. What part of the house is not painted?   •   • $\frac{1}{3}$ $\frac{2}{3}$ $\frac{3}{4}$

2. 1/3 of the circle house is painted blue. What part of the house is not painted?   •   • $\frac{1}{2}$ $\frac{1}{3}$ $\frac{1}{4}$

3. 1/4 of the square house is painted purple. What part of the house is not painted?   •   • $\frac{1}{3}$ $\frac{1}{2}$ $\frac{2}{3}$

4. 2/3 of the triangle house is painted orange. What part of the house is not painted?   •   • $\frac{1}{4}$ $\frac{1}{2}$ $\frac{2}{3}$

5. 3/4 of the hexagon house is painted green. What part of the house is not painted?   •   • $\frac{1}{4}$ $\frac{1}{3}$ $\frac{3}{4}$

28.5 Problem Solving

112

Name: _____ Date: _____

Time to the Hour

Can you help tell the story of Elmer the Elephant's journey to visit more of his jungle friends? Change the clocks below to show the time at different parts of Elmer's journey. Make sure you draw both the hour hand and the minute hand for the analog clock.

Example:

Elmer the Elephant ate snack at 3 o'clock.
Show the time on both clocks below. Draw hands on the analog clock, and write numbers on the digital clock.

3:00

1. Elmer the Elephant left his home at 1 o'clock.
Show the time on both clocks below. Draw hands on the analog clock, and write numbers on the digital clock.

29.1 Time to the Hour

2. Elmer the Elephant talked with Sara the Snake at 4 o'clock.
   Show the time on both clocks below. Draw hands on the analog clock, and write numbers on the digital clock.

3. Elmer the Elephant laughed with Henry the Hyena at 5 o'clock.
   Show the time on both clocks below. Draw hands on the analog clock, and write numbers on the digital clock.

4. Elmer the Elephant relaxed with Seth the Sloth at 7 o'clock.
   Show the time on both clocks below. Draw hands on the analog clock, and write numbers on the digital clock.

29.1 Time to the Hour

5. Elmer the Elephant finally made it home to his family at 8 o'clock.
   Show the time on both clocks below. Draw hands on the analog clock, and write numbers on the digital clock.

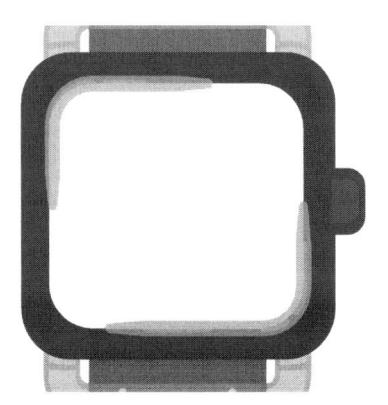

Challenge Question:

Elmer was on his journey from 1:00 to 8:00. How many hours did Elmer spend visiting his jungle friends? _____

29.1 Time to the Hour

Name: _____ Date: _____

Telling Time to the Half Hour

Can you draw the hands on the clock to show the time?

Example
9:00   6:00    9:30

2:30    10:30    4:00

12:30    7:00 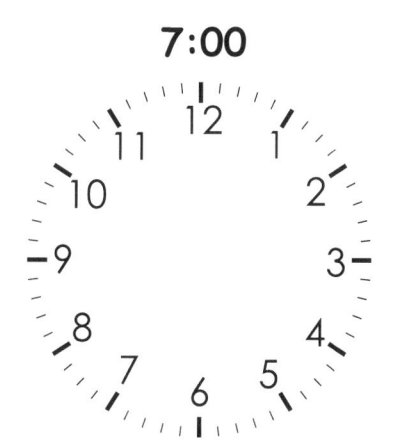   3:30

29.2 Time to the Half Hour

116

Name: _____ Date: _____

Time to the Quarter Hour

Draw lines to match each clock with the correct time to the quarter hour.

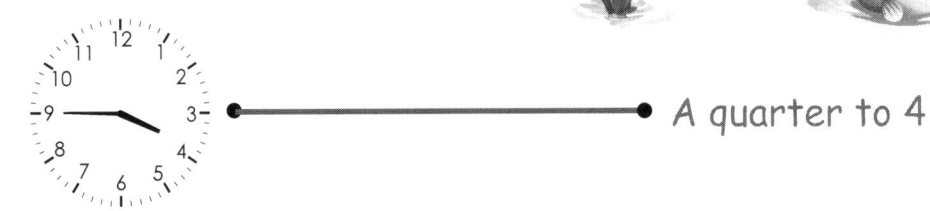

Example

- A quarter to 4

- A quarter to 9

- A quarter after 1

- A quarter to 5

- A quarter after 5

- A quarter to 1

- A quarter past 9

117

29.3 Time to the Quarter Hour

Name: _____ Date: _____

Tell the Time to 5-minutes
Draw a line matching the digital time to the analog clock.

• 5:50

• 6:40

• 3:55

• 10:05

• 1:30

• 9:20

29.4 Time to Five-Minute Intervals

118

Name: _____ Date: _____

Tell the Time
Draw the hour hand and minute hand on the clock to show the elapsed time.

Example

Draw the time it will be 2 hours later than 3:00. You got it! It's 5 o'clock.

1. What time will it be in 2 hours?

2. What time will it be in 4 hours?

3. What time will it be in 3 hours?

119

29.5 Tell the Time

Next page

4. What time will it be in 2 hours?

5. What time will it be in 3 hours?

6. What time will it be in 2 hours?

29.5 Tell the Time

120

Problem Solving: Find a Pattern Telling Time

Draw the hands on the blank clock to show the time pattern.

Example

1.

2.

3.

4.

121

30.2 Problem Solving: Find a Pattern

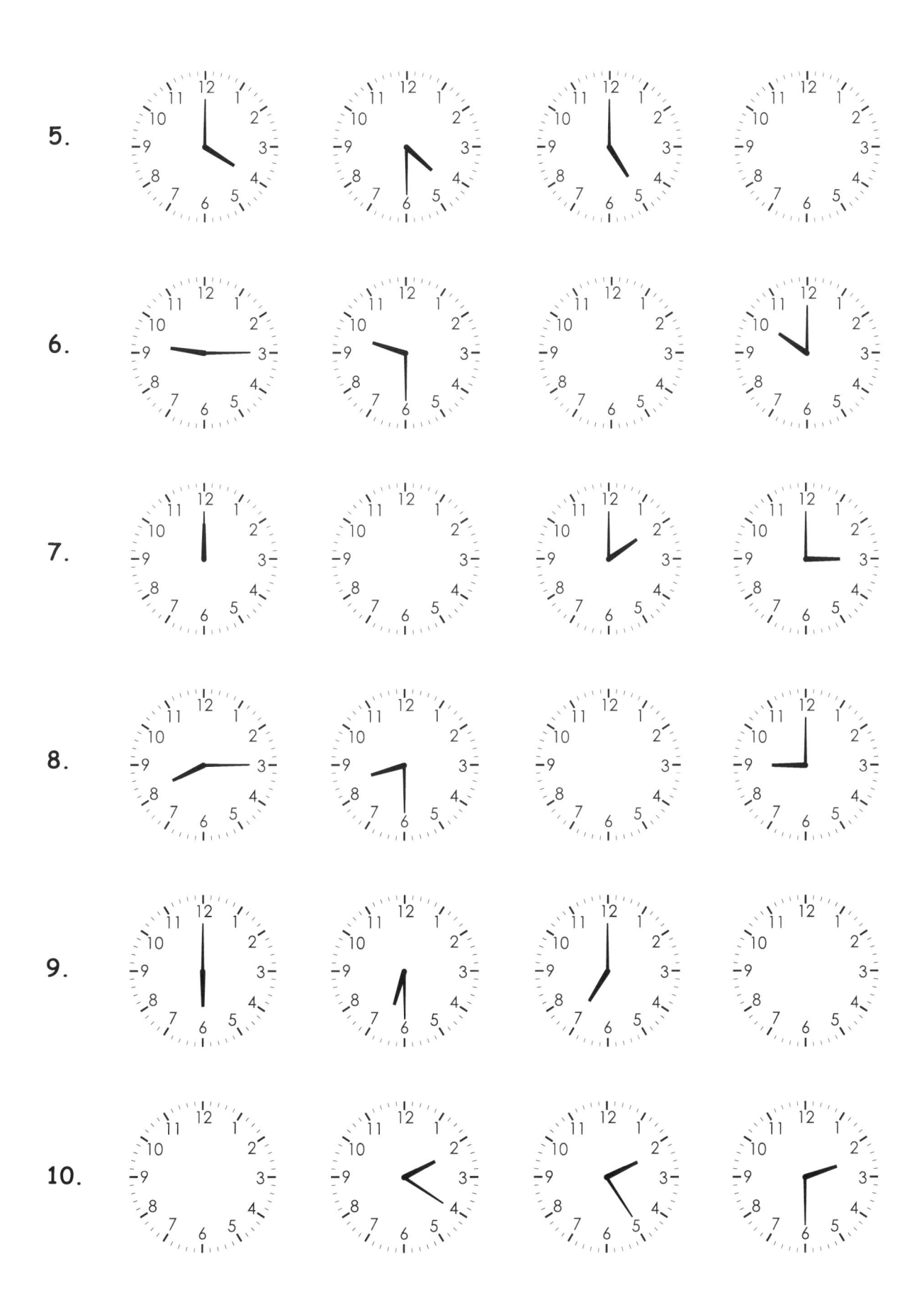

5.

6.

7.

8.

9.

10.

30.2 Problem Solving: Find a Pattern 122

Name: _____ Date: _____

Word Problems: Time

Read the word problem. Draw the hands on the clock to show the answer. Write the answer on the space provided. Remember to include A.M. or P.M.

Example

Mr. Owl listened to campers telling campfire stories. The campers started at 9 o'clock that evening and finished 2 hours later. What time did the campers finish telling campfire stories?

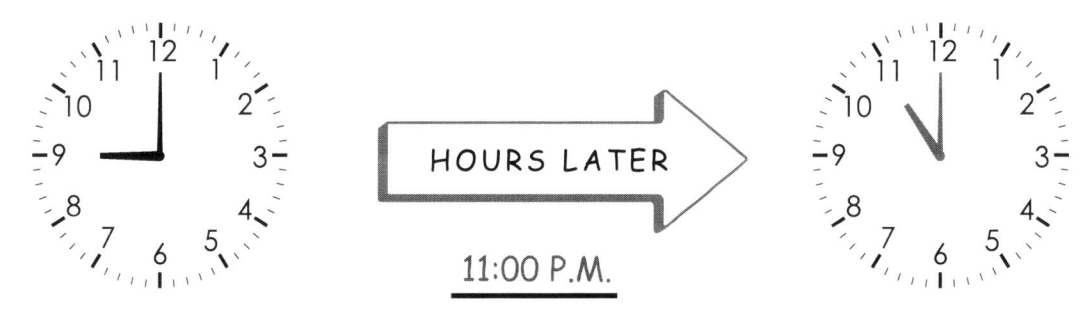

HOURS LATER

11:00 P.M.

1. Mr. Owl watched campers set up their tents for 2 hours beginning at 8 o'clock in the morning. What time did the campers finish setting up their tents?

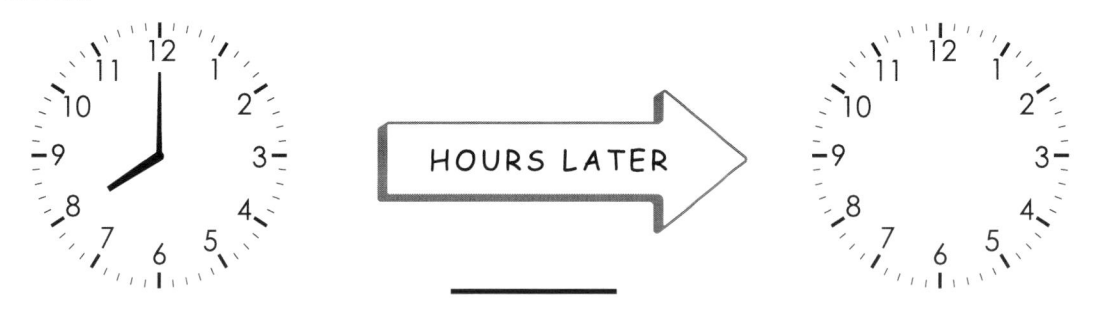

    HOURS LATER

    _____

2. Campers played hide-and-seek in the forest for 15 minutes starting at 1:30 in the afternoon. What time did the campers finish playing hide-and-seek?

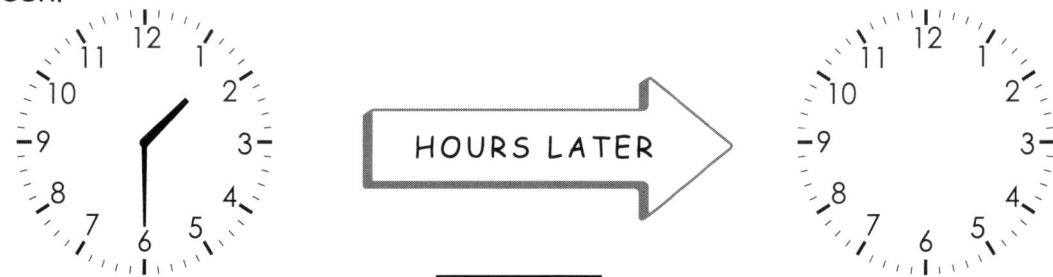

    HOURS LATER

    _____

123

30.3 Word Problems: Time

Next page

3. Campers made s'mores starting at 7 o'clock that evening and finished a half an hour, or 30 minutes, later. What time did the campers finish their s'mores?

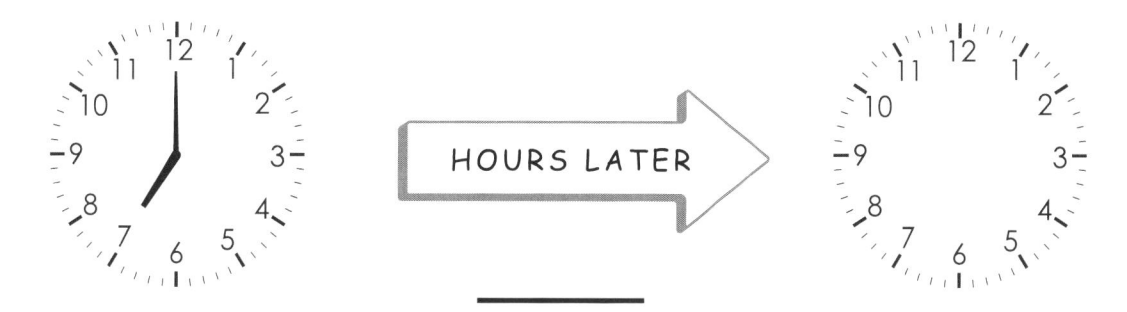

4. Campers started a hike after breakfast at 10:15 and hiked for 45 minutes all the way to the top of the mountain. What time did the campers reach the top of the mountain?

5. Mr. Owl watched the campers fishing. The campers started fishing at 12 o'clock, or noon, and finished 2 hours later. What time did the campers finish fishing?

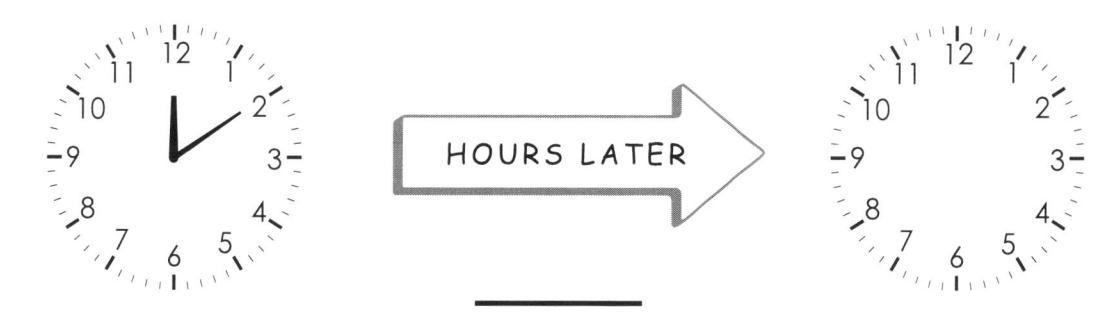

30.3 Word Problems: Time

Name: _____ Date: _____

Compare Time: Earlier and Later

Draw the time on the clocks showing earlier and later times of day.

Example

〈〈 1 hour earlier   1 hour later 〉〉

1.

〈〈 3 hours earlier   3 hours later 〉〉

2.

〈〈 30 min earlier   30 min later 〉〉

3.

〈〈 15 min earlier   15 min later 〉〉

30.4 Compare Times

4. 2 hours earlier — 6:00 — 2 hours later

5. 2 hours earlier — 1:00 — 2 hours later

6. 3 hours earlier — 7:00 — 3 hours later

30.4 Compare Times

Name: _____ Date: _____

Measuring Time

Mark the best estimate of time needed for each activity.

Example:

brushing your teeth

- ☐ 1 week
- ☐ 1 month
- ☑ 1 minute

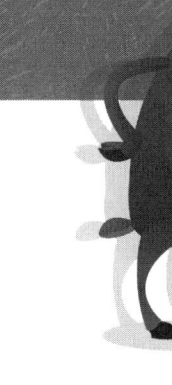

1. reading a bedtime story

   - ☐ 15 days
   - ☐ 15 minutes
   - ☐ 15 hours

2. watching a movie with your family

   - ☐ 2 hours
   - ☐ 2 minutes
   - ☐ 2 days

3. enjoying summer vacation!

   - ☐ 2 months
   - ☐ 2 days
   - ☐ 2 hours

4. building a new house

   - ☐ 1 year
   - ☐ 1 hour
   - ☐ 1 month

5. taking an afternoon nap
- ☐ 2 days
- ☐ 2 weeks
- ☐ 2 hours

6. building a snowman
- ☐ 1 day
- ☐ 1 hour
- ☐ 1 minute

7. cleaning your room
- ☐ 30 days
- ☐ 30 hours
- ☐ 30 minutes

8. celebrating your birthday
- ☐ 1 month
- ☐ 1 year
- ☐ 1 day

9. shopping for groceries with your family
- ☐ 2 days
- ☐ 2 minutes
- ☐ 2 hours

10. spending an afternoon at the swimming pool
- ☐ 3 hours
- ☐ 3 days
- ☐ 3 minutes

30.5 Measuring Time

Name: _____ Date: _____

Measurement Data

Wit the Robot is finding all the best treats in the city! Find the total number of each kind of bakery and ice cream treat. Write the tally mark data.

Wit the Robot's Visit to the Bakery

Bakery Treat	Total Number of Bakery Treats	Tally Marks
Example:	7	||||| ||
	____	
	____	
	____	
	____	

129

32.1 Measurement Data

Wit the Robot's Visit to the Ice Cream Parlor

Ice Cream Treat	Total	Tally Marks
	_____	
	_____	
	_____	
	_____	

32.1 Measurement Data

130

Name: _____ Date: _____

Make and Analyze a Line Plot

Q the Robot loves Central Park! He has gathered data from the people who are riding their bikes around the park! Central Park is 5 miles long, but not all of the people travel the full length of the park. Let's gather the data and make a line plot to show how far they traveled.

Complete the tally mark data and line plot graph. Fill in the Xs on the line plot to show the number of bicyclists, or people riding bicycles, and how many miles they traveled in the park.

Miles Traveled	Number of Bicyclists	Tally Marks
5 miles	5 bicyclists	
4 miles	10 bicyclists	
3 miles	11 bicyclists	
2 miles	8 bicyclists	
1 mile	15 bicyclists	|||| |||| ||||

Miles Traveled by Bicyclists

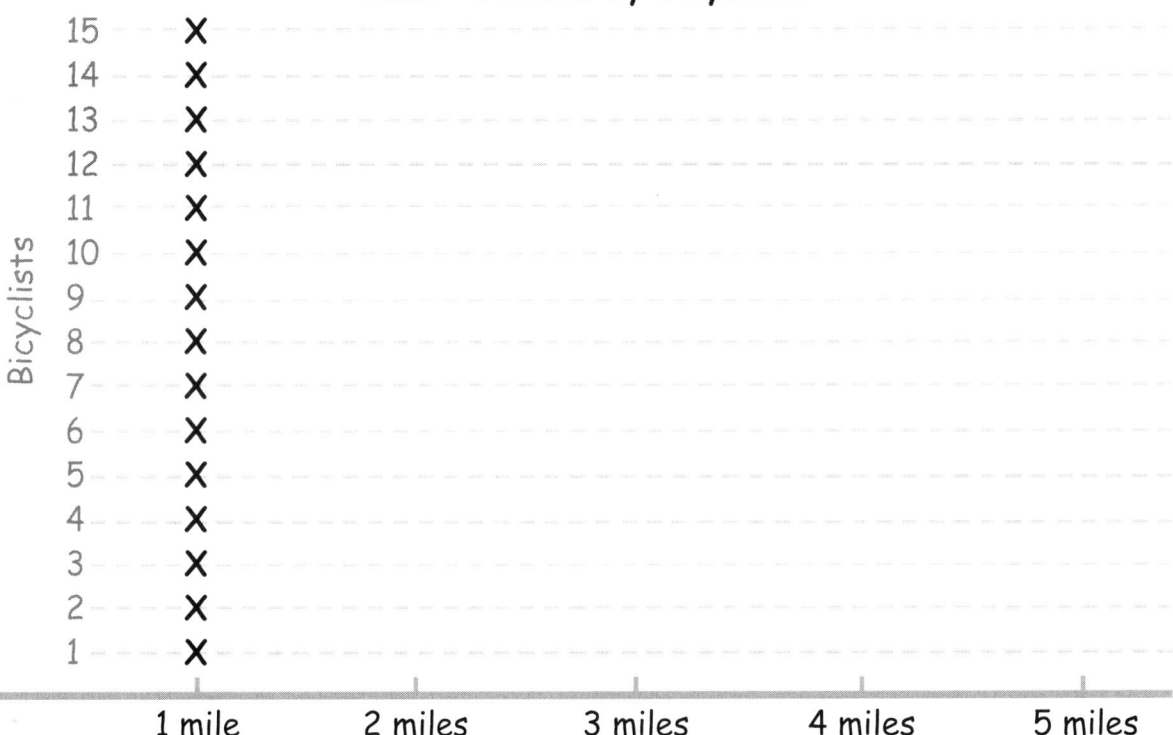

```
15 --X
14 --X
13 --X
12 --X
11 --X
10 --X
 9 --X
 8 --X
 7 --X
 6 --X
 5 --X
 4 --X
 3 --X
 2 --X
 1 --X
     1 mile   2 miles   3 miles   4 miles   5 miles
```
Bicyclists

131   32.2 Make and Analyze Line Plots

Let's analyze the data! Answer the following questions.

What is the title of the graph?

What are the top two categories that were traveled by the bicyclists?

What is the fewest number of miles that the bicyclists traveled?

How many miles did 10 bicyclists travel?

How many total bicyclists are there in Q's data?

32.2 Make and Analyze Line Plots

Name: _____ Date: _____

Make and Analyze a Bar Graph

Dot the Robot has gathered data from the city students about their favorite lunch foods! Complete the tally mark data and bar graph. Color in the bar graph to show the lunch favorites.

Lunch Favorites	Total Number of Students	Tally Marks
 Example: Hot Dogs	6	|||||	
 Pizza	10	
 Chicken Nuggets	8	
 Sandwich	5	
 Soup	3	

133

32.4 Make and Analyze Bar Graphs

Next page

Lunch Favorites

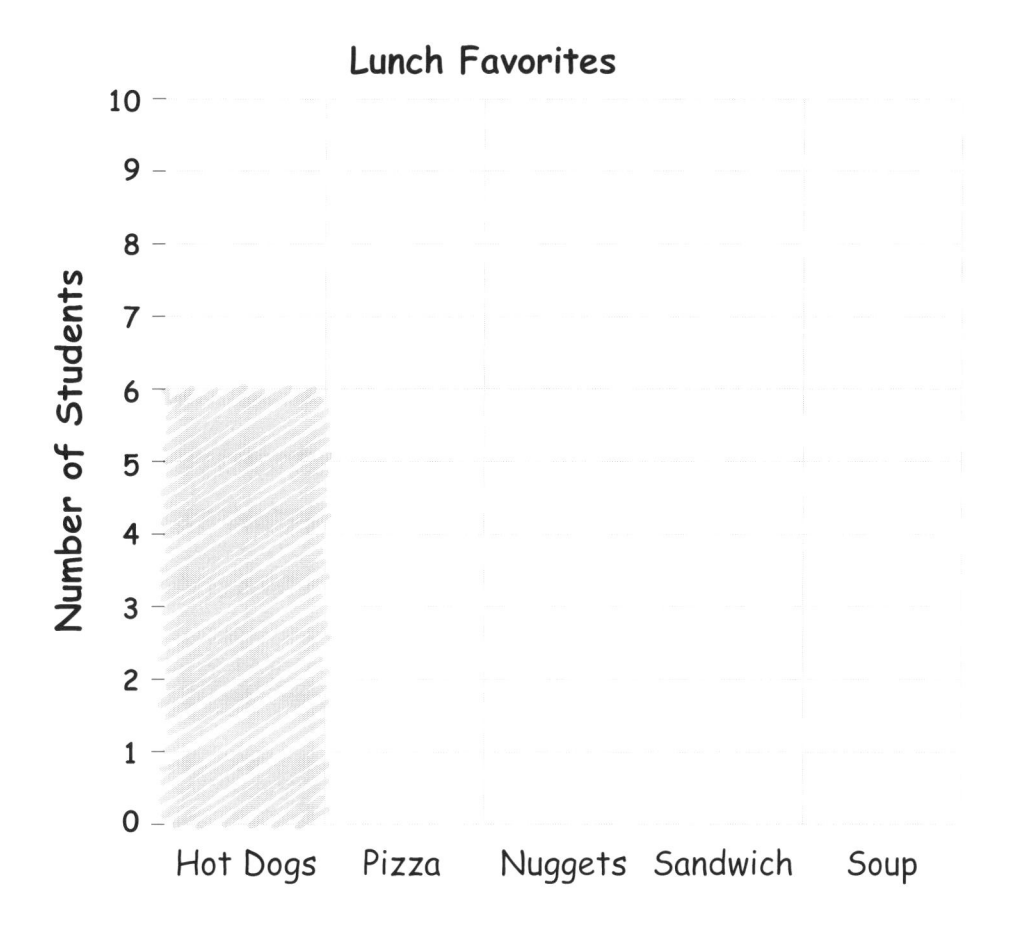

(Bar graph: Number of Students (y-axis, 0–10) vs Hot Dogs, Pizza, Nuggets, Sandwich, Soup. Hot Dogs bar = 6.)

Let's analyze the data! Answer the following questions.

1. What is the title of the bar graph?

2. Which foods are the top two favorites of the city students?

3. Which lunch is the city students' least favorite?

4. Which lunch favorite is liked by 5 students?

5. How many more students like pizza than like soup?

Name: _____ Date: _____

Problem Solving with Graphs

Tank the Robot collected data of the students' favorite drinks. Fill in the tally mark data chart.

Subway Drinks	Total Number of Students	Tally Marks
 Hot Chocolate	5	
 Iced Tea	8	
 Water	3	
 Soda	10	

32.5 Problem Solving

Use the tally mark data to create a line plot graph and bar graph. Use crayons or pencils to add the data.

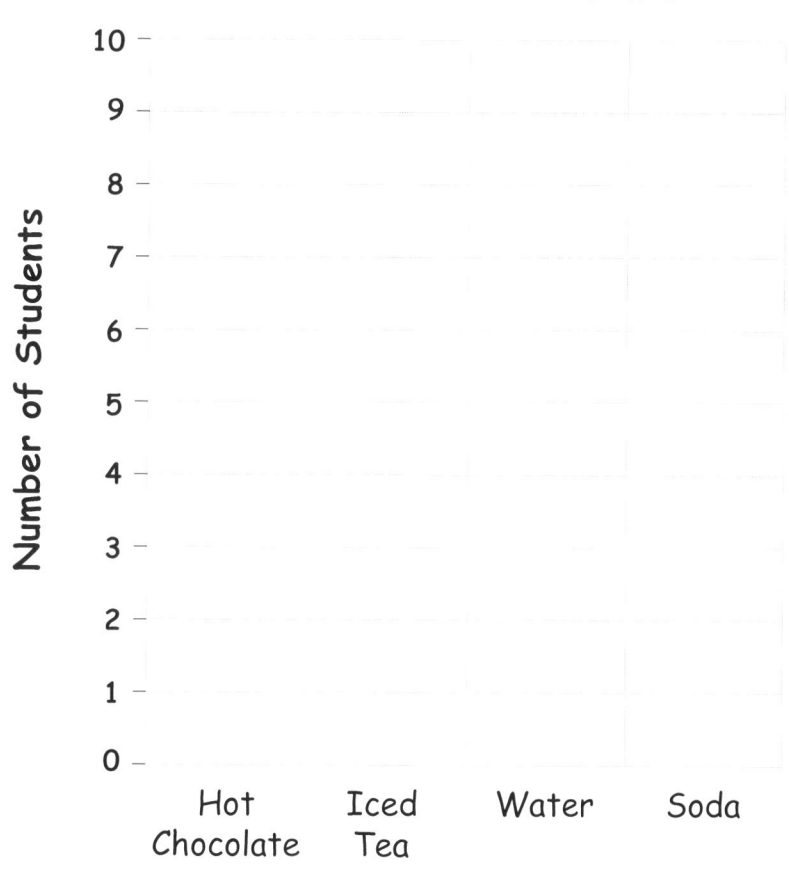

Student's Favorite Drinks

(Graph: y-axis "Number of Students" 0–10; x-axis: Hot Chocolate, Iced Tea, Water, Soda)

Student's Favorite Drinks

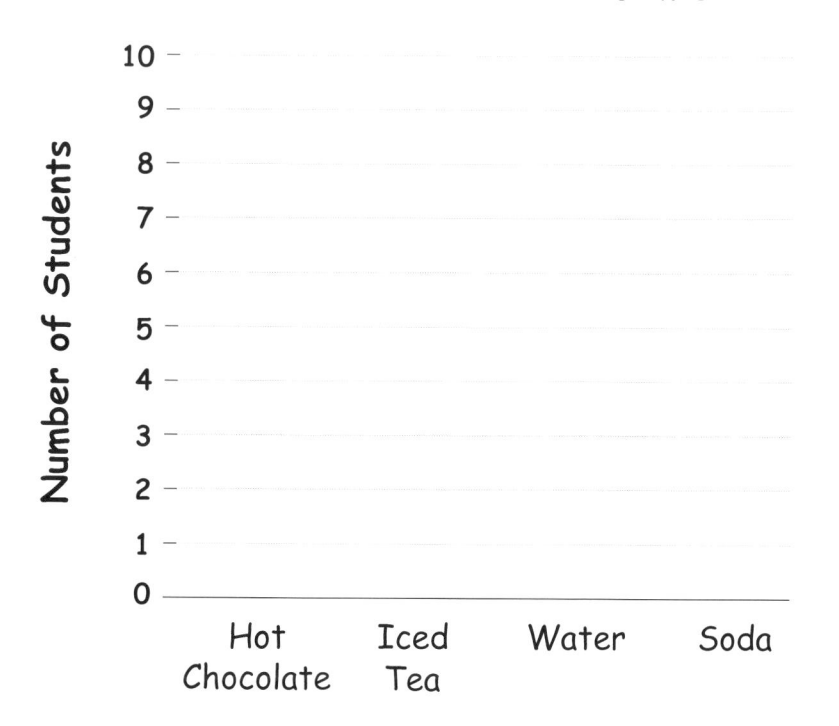

(Graph: y-axis "Number of Students" 0–10; x-axis: Hot Chocolate, Iced Tea, Water, Soda)

32.5 Problem Solving

Using the line plot or bar graph you created, answer the following questions.

1. What is the title of the line plot and bar graph?

2. What was the most favorite drink of the students?

3. What was the least favorite drink?

4. How many students total had drinks?

Name: _____ Date: _____

Counting Equal Groups

How many ice cream treats can you count? Let's look at an example of multiplication and repeated addition.

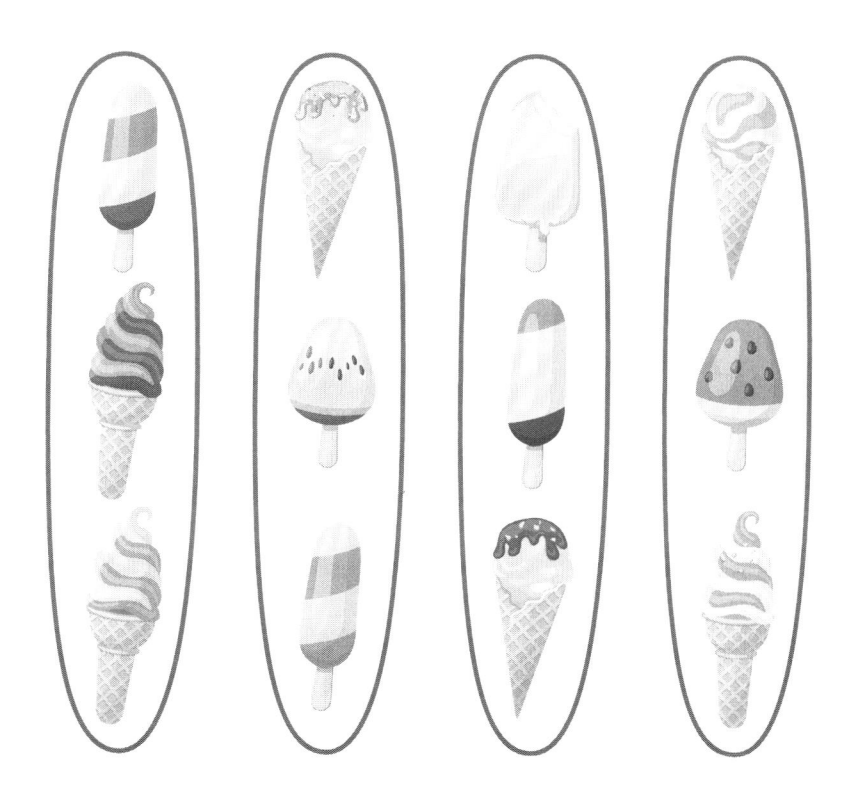

There are **4 groups** of ice cream treats.

There are **3 in each group**.

You can add by using repeated addition: **3 + 3 + 3 + 3 = 12**.

You can multiply 4 groups of 3: **4 × 3 = 12**.

33.1 Multiplication

Next page

Complete the multiplication and repeated addition. Fill in the missing blanks.

1.

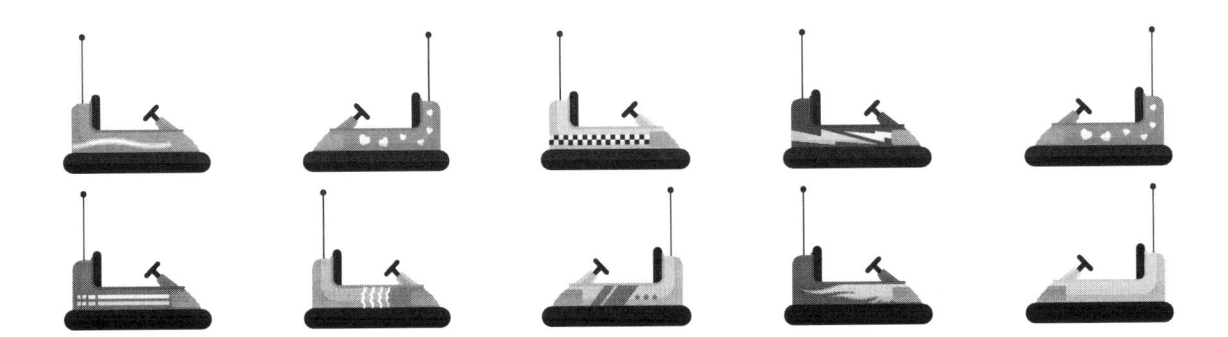

- 5 groups of _____

- 2 + _____ + _____ + _____ + _____ = _____

- 5 x _____ = _____

2.

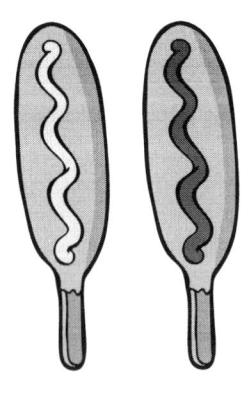

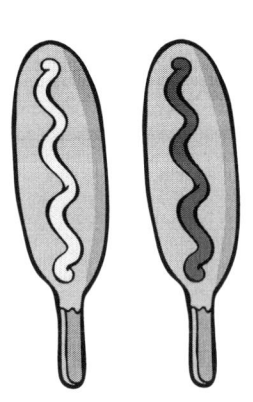

- 2 groups of _____

- 2 + _____ = _____

- 2 x _____ = _____

139

33.1 Multiplication

3.

- 2 groups of _____

- 3 + _____ = _____

- 2 × _____ = _____

4.

- 4 groups of _____

- 3 + _____ + _____ + _____ = _____

- 4 × _____ = _____

33.1 Multiplication

5.

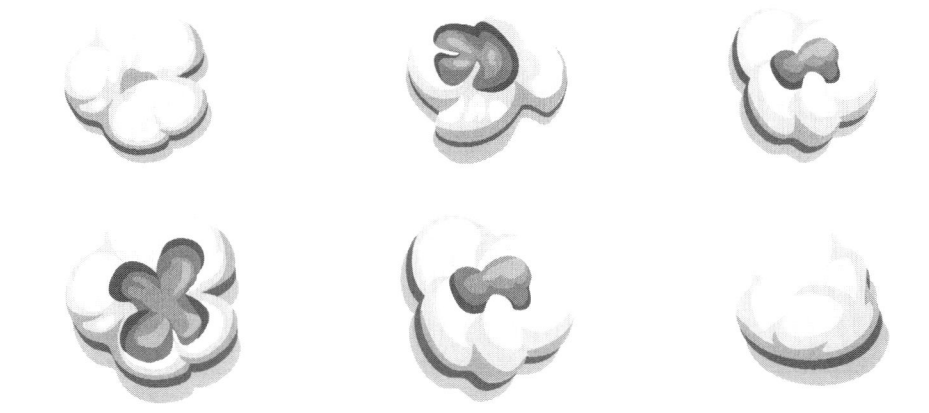

- 3 groups of _____
- 2 + _____ + _____ = _____
- 3 × _____ = _____

6.

- 2 groups of _____
- 6 + _____ = _____
- 2 × _____ = _____

33.1 Multiplication

Name: _____ Date: _____

Multiplication at the Petting Zoo

Fill in the blanks.

1.

1 group of 9 bunnies

1 × ___ = 9 bunnies

2.

1 group of ___ sheep

1 × ___ = ___ sheep

33.2 Multiply by Ones

142

Next page

3.

1 group of ___ goats

1 x ___ = ___ goats

4.

___ group of 8 ducks

___ x 8 = ___ ducks

5.

___ group of 5 ponies

___ x 5 = ___ ponies

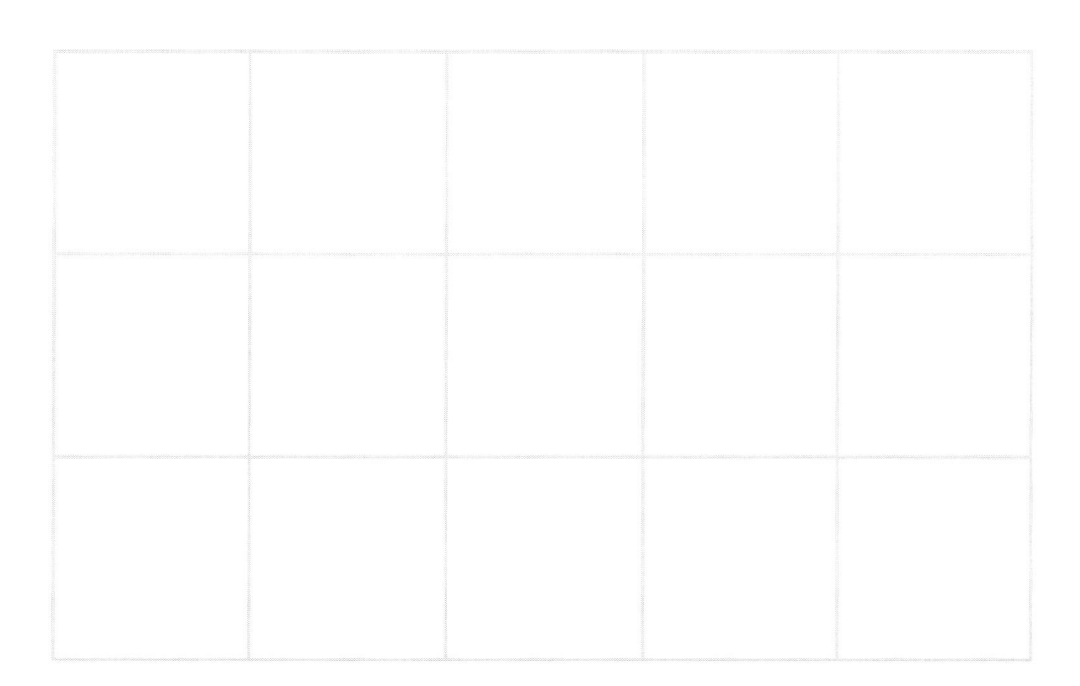

Fill In and Multiply

Use a crayon to fill in the boxes with dots to create arrays. Then, write multiplication and addition sentences to solve the problems in the lesson.

_____ x _____ = _____

_____ + _____ + _____ = _____

33.3 Multiply with Arrays

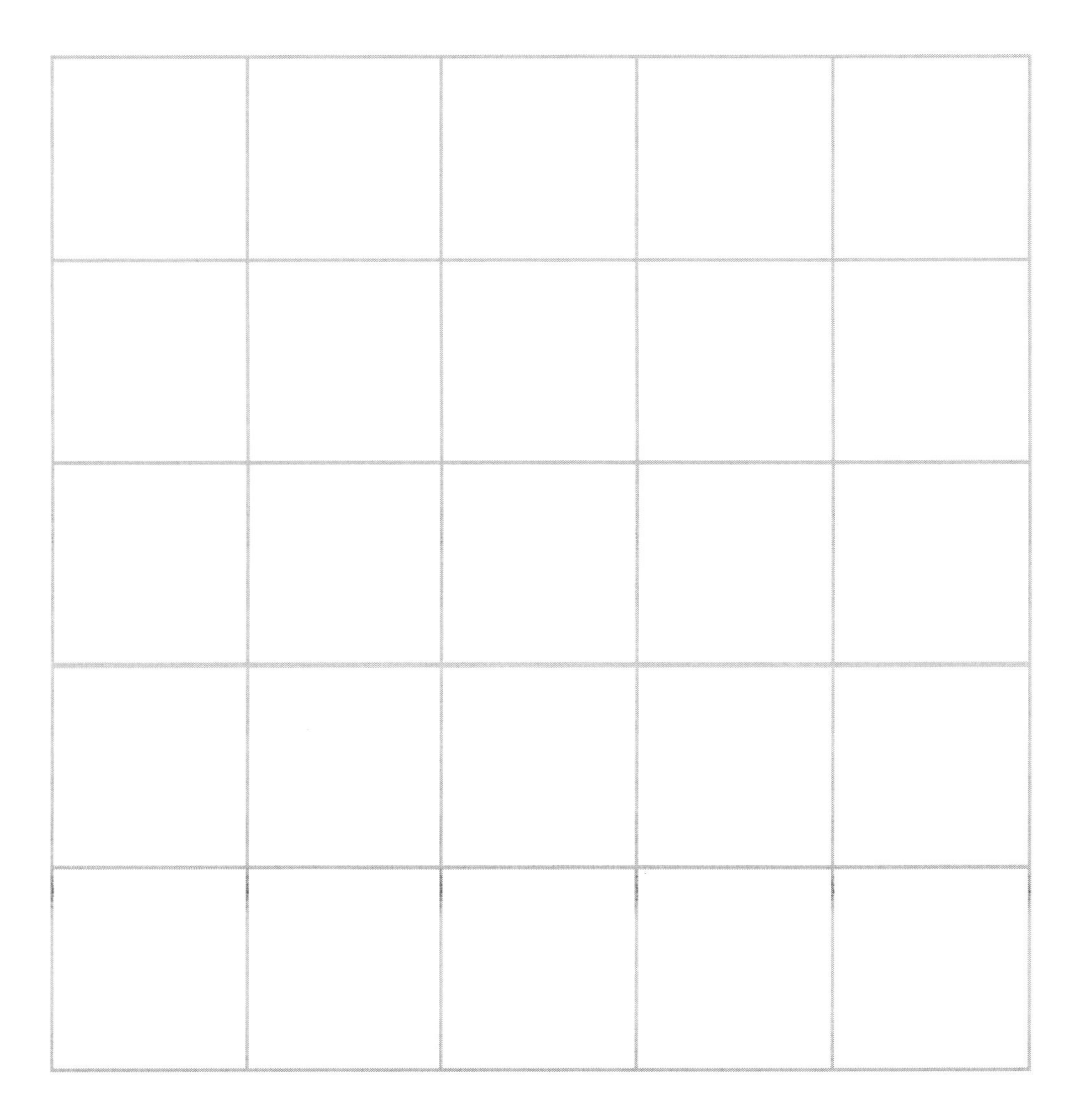

_____ × _____ = _____

_____ + _____ + _____ + _____ + _____ = _____

145 33.3 Multiply with Arrays

Name: _____ Date: _____

Array Match and Multiply

Match the array to the correct multiplication sentence. Then, fill in the repeated addend and find the answer!

Example:

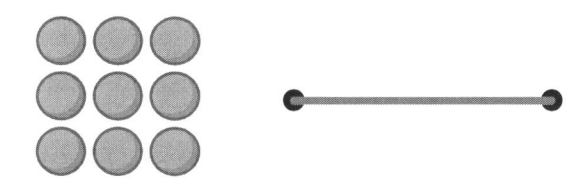

3 × 3 = ?
_3_ + _3_ + _3_ = _9_

2 × 3 = ?
___ + ___ = ___

5 × 2 = ?
___ + ___ + ___ + ___ + ___ = ___

3 × 4 = ?
___ + ___ + ___ = ___

4 × 5 = ?
___ + ___ + ___ + ___ = ___

4 × 4 = ?
___ + ___ + ___ + ___ = ___

33.3 Multiply with Arrays

Name: _____ Date: _____

Multiply by Adding

Find the numbers for each multiplication sentence. Draw counters in the circles to create a picture for each multiplication sentence. Use your pictures to find the answer!

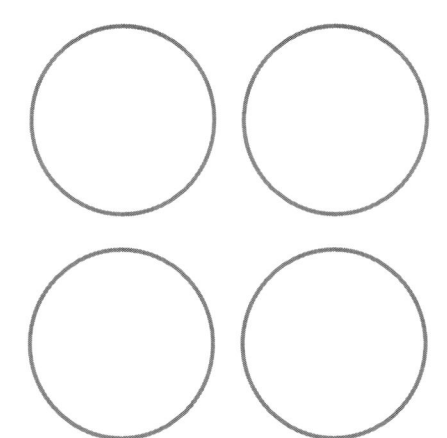

3 + 3 + 3 + 3 + 3 = ?

____ × ____ = ____

5 + 5 + 5 + 5 = ?

____ × ____ = ____

147

33.4 Multiply by Adding

Name: _____ Date: _____

Add to Multiply

Use the repeated addition and multiplication sentences to help you draw a multiplication picture in the circles. Then, find the answer and write it on the line.

Example:

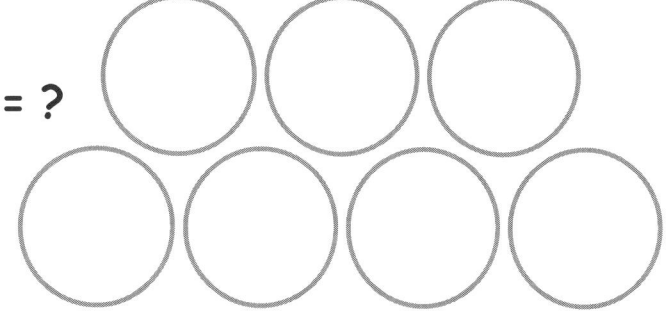

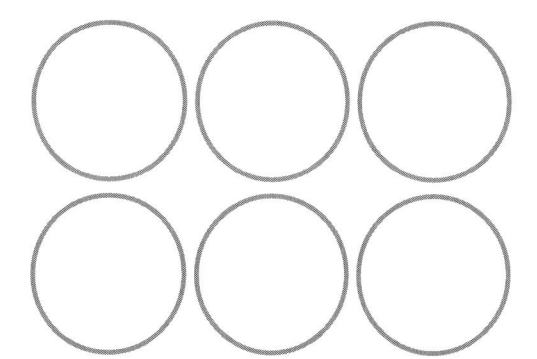

6 + 6 + 6 + 6 = ?

4 × 6 = __24__

1 + 1 + 1 + 1 + 1 + 1 + 1 = ?

7 × 1 = ____

2 + 2 + 2 + 2 + 2 + 2 = ?

6 × 2 = ____

33.4 Multiply by Adding

148

Next page

3 + 3 + 3 + 3 + 3 = ?

5 × 3 = ____

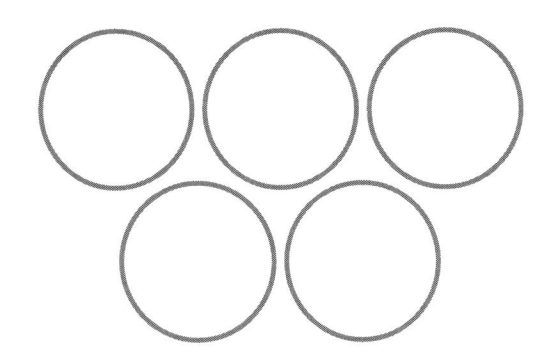

4 + 4 + 4 = ?

3 × 4 = ____

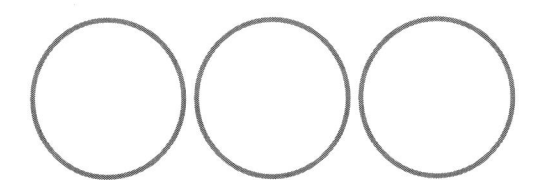

5 + 5 + 5 + 5 + 5 = ?

5 × 5 = ____

33.4 Multiply by Adding

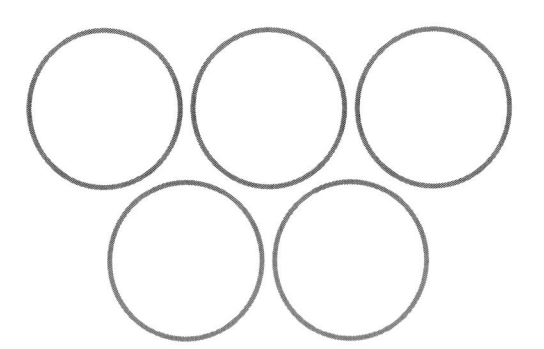

Name: _____ Date: _____

Inner Tube Match!

Let's ride the water slide! Circle the correct multiplication or repeated addition sentence. Find each answer and write it on the line.

Example: _6_

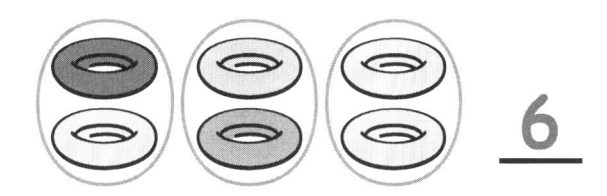

4 x 2 = ?   3 x 3 = ?   (3 x 2 = ?)

___

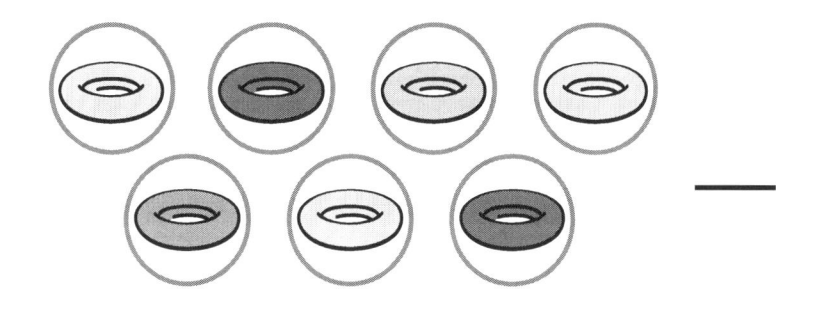

7 x 1 = ?   6 x 1 = ?   5 x 1 = ?

___

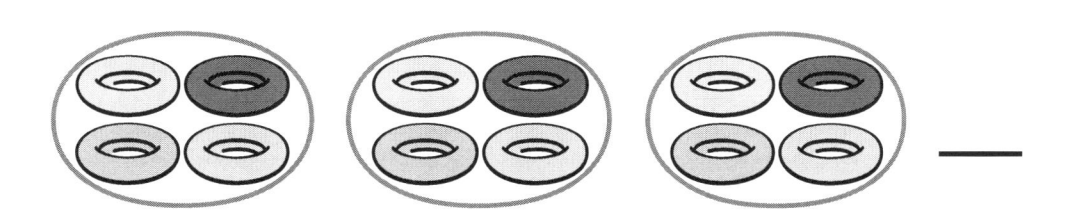

3 + 3 + 3 = ?   4 + 4 + 4 = ?   4 + 4 = ?

33.5 Multiplication Matching

150

Next page

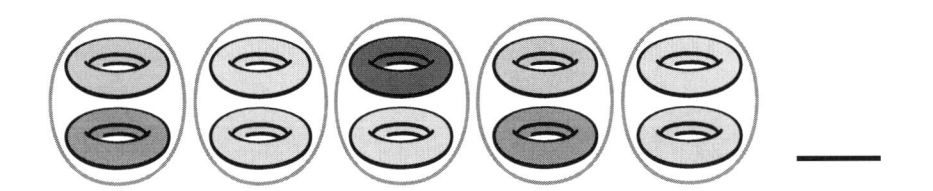

5 + 5 + 5 + 5 + 5 = ?   2 + 2 + 2 + 2 = ?   2 + 2 + 2 + 2 + 2 = ?

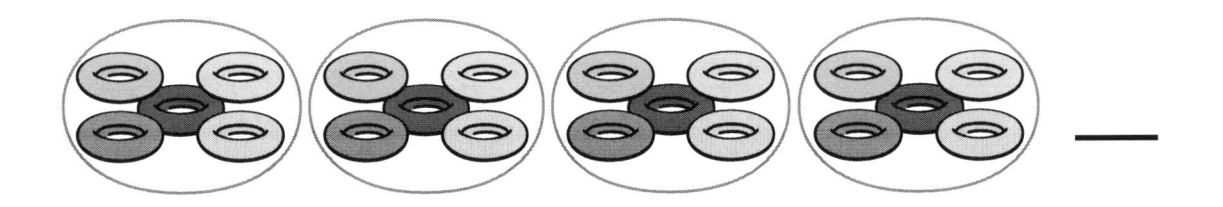

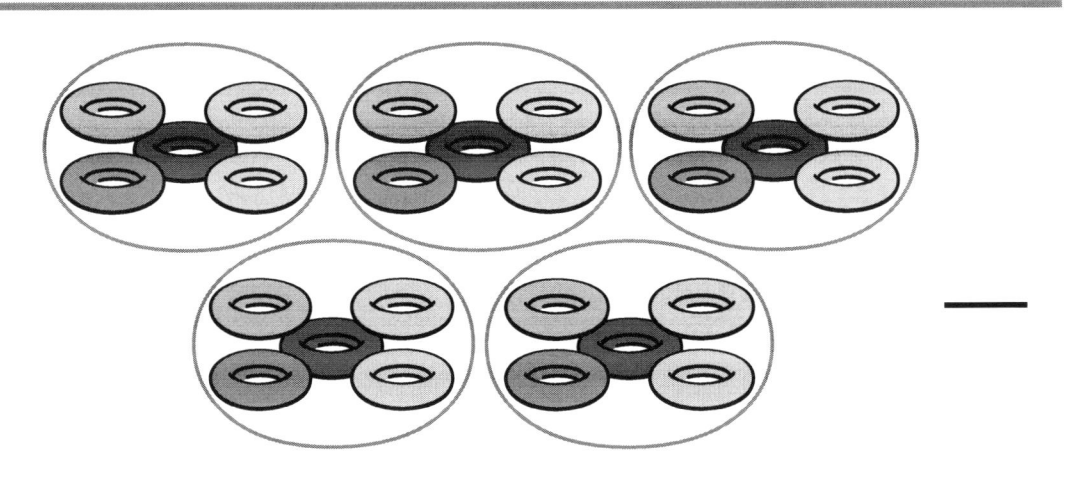

4 × 4 = ?   4 × 5 = ?   5 × 3 = ?

4 × 4 = ?   4 × 5 = ?   5 × 5 = ?

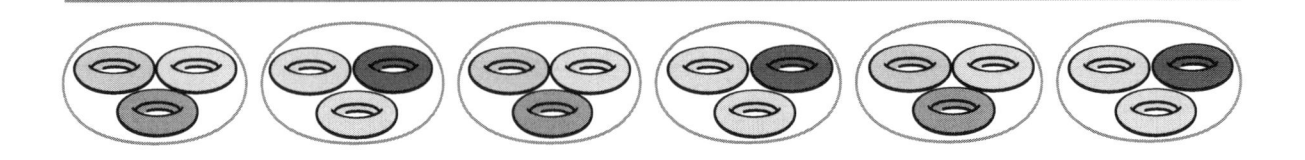

3 + 3 + 3 + 3 + 3 + 3 = ?   6 + 6 + 6 + 6 = ?   3 + 3 + 3 + 3 + 3 = ?

33.5 Multiplication Matching

Name: _____ Date: _____

Array Skip Counting

Use your counters to make each array. Draw a dot under each counter. Skip count by 2s and write each number on the line. Then, write the total number in each box!

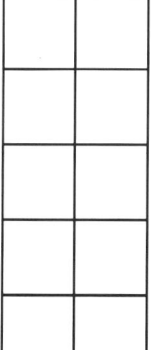

__ , __ , __ , __ , __ , __ , __ , __

2 + 2 + 2 + 2 + 2 + 2 + 2 + 2 = ☐

8 × 2 = ☐

__ , __ , __ , __ , __ , __ , __ , __ , __ , __

2 + 2 + 2 + 2 + 2 + 2 + 2 + 2 + 2 + 2 = ☐

10 × 2 = ☐

34.1 Skip Counting by 2s

152

Name: _____ Date: _____

Array Match and Multiply

Match the array to the correct multiplication sentence. Then, fill in the answer!

Example:

2 + 2 = ?
2 × 2 = _4_

1.

2 + 2 + 2 + 2 = ?
4 × 2 = ___

2.

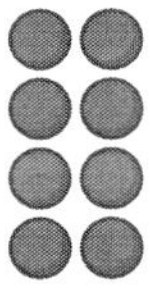

2 + 2 + 2 = ?
3 × 2 = ___

3.

2+2+2+2+2+2+2+2+2+2=?
10 × 2 = ___

4.

2 + 2 + 2 + 2 + 2 + 2 + 2 = ?
7 × 2 = ___

5.

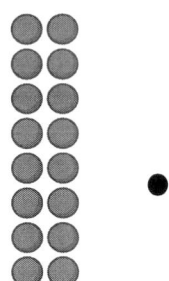

2+2+2+2+2+2+2+2+2=?
9 × 2 = ___

153

34.1 Skip Counting by 2s

Name: _____ Date: _____

Draw to Skip Count

Draw dots in the boxes to create each array. Skip count by 5s and write the numbers on the lines. Then write the total number in the boxes!

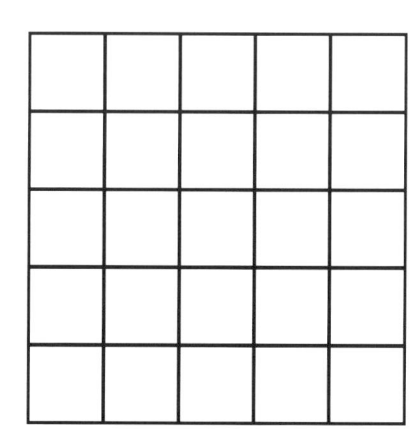

___ , ___ , ___

5 + 5 + 5 = ☐

3 × 5 = ☐

___ , ___ , ___ , ___ , ___

5 + 5 + 5 + 5 + 5 = ☐

5 × 5 = ☐

34.2 Skip Counting by 5s

154

Name: _____ Date: _____

Skip Count and Color

Skip count by 5s to find the total, and write it on the line. Then, look at the game board and color each space the correct color.

5 + 5 = ?

2 × 5 = ___

BLUE

5 + 5 + 5 = ?

3 × 5 = ___

ORANGE

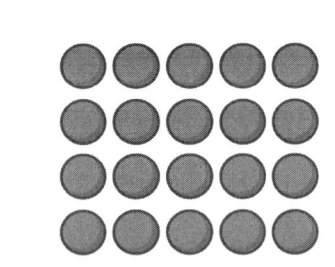

5 + 5 + 5 + 5 = ?

4 × 5 = ___

RED

5 + 5 + 5 + 5 + 5 = ?

5 × 5 = ___

GREEN

155

34.2 Skip Counting by 5s

Next pag

Color the game board like you would a coloring book page. Use the list below and your answers from the previous page to color each category the correct color.

Numbers: 10
Head and even spaces: 15
Tongue and odd spaces: 20
Grass: 25

34.2 Skip Counting by 5s

Name: _____ Date: _____

Draw to Skip Count

Draw each array in the box. Skip count by 10s, and write the numbers on the lines. Then write the total number in the boxes!

__ , __ , __ , __

10+10+10+10 = ☐

4 × 10 = ☐

__ , __ , __ , __ , __

10+10+10+10+10 = ☐

5 × 10 = ☐

157

34.3 Skip Counting by 10s

Name: _____ Date: _____

Multiplication Message

Skip count by 10s, and write each number on the line. Write the total number in the box. Write the correct letters on the lines that match each answer.

Example:

Put a V on the lines that have a 10 under them

<u>10</u>

10 + 0 = ?

1 × 10 = [10]

V

___,___

10 + 10 = ?

2 × 10 = ☐

S

___,___,___

10 + 10 + 10 = ?

3 × 10 = ☐

N

___,___,___,___

10 + 10 + 10 + 10 = ?

4 × 10 = ☐

A

34.3 Skip Counting by 10s

158

Next page

10 + 10 + 10 + 10 + 10 = ?

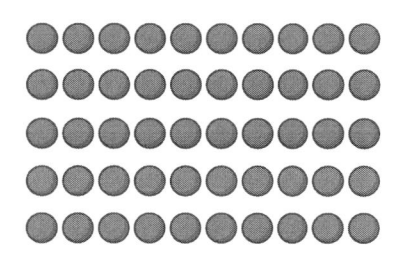

5 × 10 = ☐   E

Why was 6 afraid of 7?

B __ C __ U __ __ __ V __ __ __ __ T __ __ I __ __
 50   40   20 50 20 50 10 50 30 40 50 30 30 50

159 34.3 Skip Counting by 10s

Name: _____ Date: _____

Array and Skip-Counting Sheet

You will match multiplication sentences to total numbers. It is up to you if you would like to use this sheet. Draw arrays and skip count below when you need to!

___

10 + 0 = ☐

1 × 10 = ☐

___ , ___

10 + 10 = ☐

2 × 10 = ☐

34.3 Skip Counting by 10s

160

Next page

___, ___, ___

10 + 10 + 10 = ☐

3 × 10 = ☐

___, ___, ___, ___

10 + 10 + 10 + 10 = ☐

4 × 10 = ☐

___, ___, ___, ___, ___

10+10+10+10+10 = ☐

5 × 10 = ☐

34.3 Skip Counting by 10s

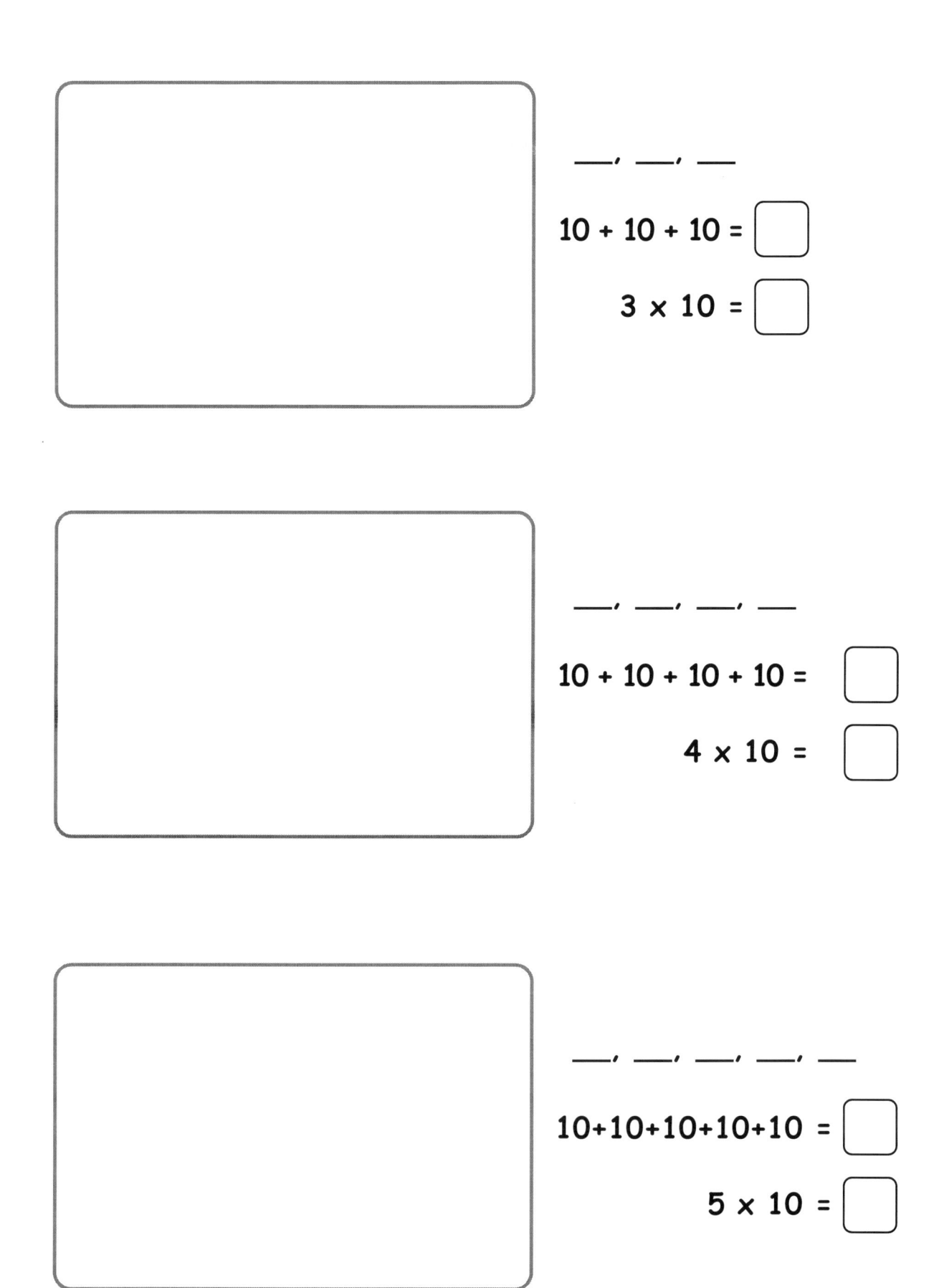

Name: _____ Date: _____

Read and Solve

Read each problem. Use the array or repeated addition sentence to solve. Write the total number in each box.

Example:

We have 3 rows with 2 blocks in each row. How many blocks do we have in all?

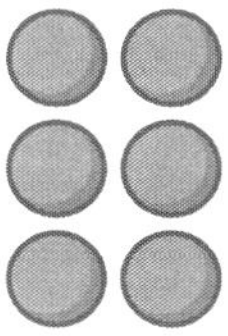

2 + 2 + 2 = [6]

3 × 2 = [6]

We have 2 rows with 5 blocks in each row. How many blocks do we have in all?

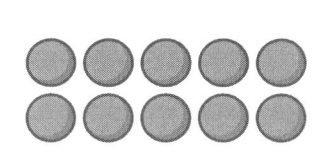

5 + 5 = [ ]

5 × 2 = [ ]

We have 5 rows with 3 blocks in each row. How many blocks do we have in all?

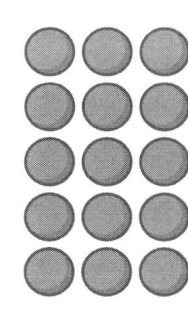

3 + 3 + 3 + 3 + 3 = [ ]

5 × 3 = [ ]

We have 4 rows with 4 blocks in each row. How many blocks do we have in all?

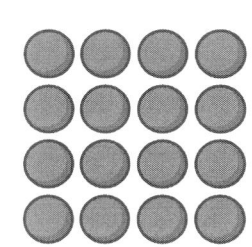

4 + 4 + 4 + 4 = [ ]

4 × 4 = [ ]

34.4 Problem Solving

Next page

We have 3 rows with 6 blocks in each row. How many blocks do we have in all?

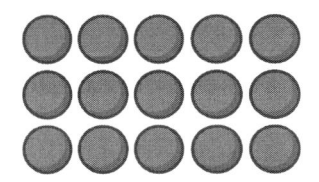

6 + 6 + 6 = ☐

3 × 6 = ☐

We have 10 rows with 2 blocks in each row. How many blocks do we have in all?

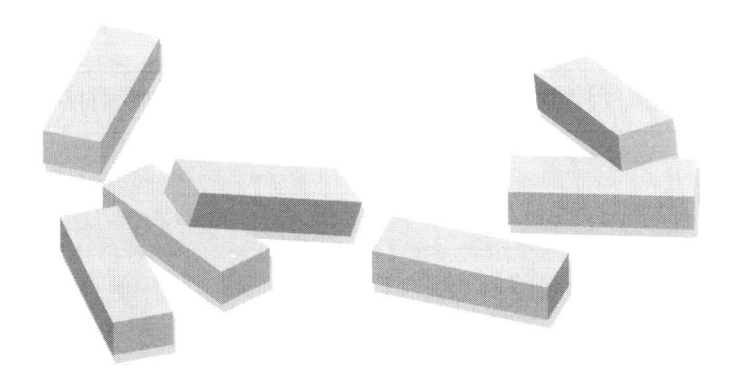

2+2+2+2+2+2+2+2+2+2 = ☐

10 × 2 = ☐

34.4 Problem Solving

Name: _____ Date: _____

Pick and Partner Solve

Pick 3 problems, and ask your partner to work on the rest. Use the picture or array to fill in the important numbers. Then, trade problems with each other to solve! Write the total number in the box.

There are __ groups of __ dice on the floor. How many dice in total do we need to put away?

$1 + 1 + 1 + 1 + 1 + 1 = ?$
$5 \times 1 = ?$

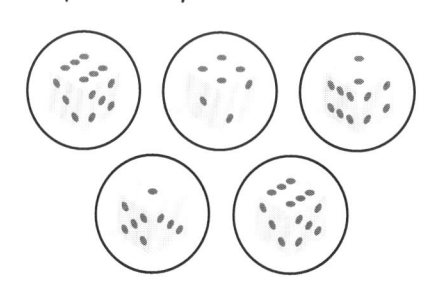

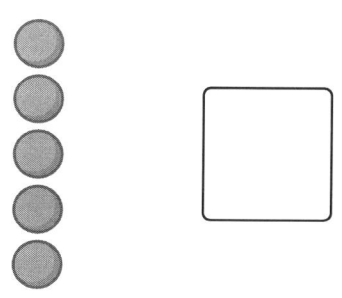

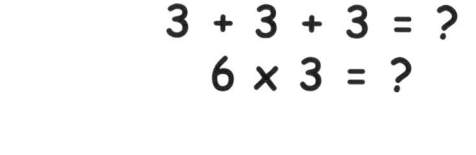

There are __ groups of __ pieces on the floor. How many pieces in total do we need to put away?

$3 + 3 + 3 = ?$
$6 \times 3 = ?$

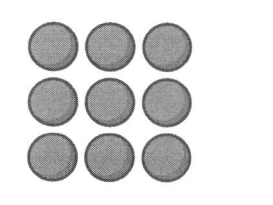

34.5 Multiplication Story Problems

There are __ piles of __ cards on the floor. How many cards in total do we need to put away?

$4 + 4 + 4 = ?$
$3 \times 4 = ?$

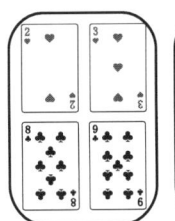

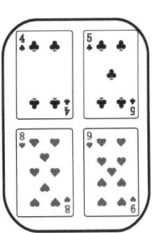

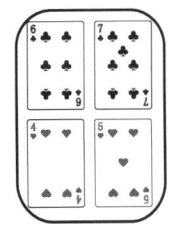

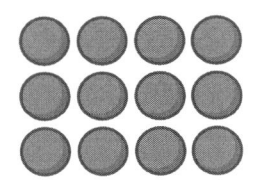

There are __ groups of __ dice on the floor. How many dice in total do we need to put away?

$2+2+2+2+2+2+2 = ?$
$3 \times 3 = ?$

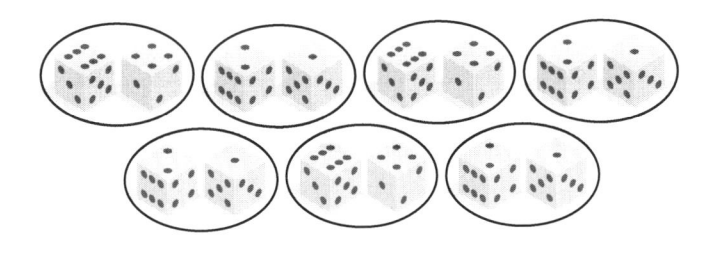

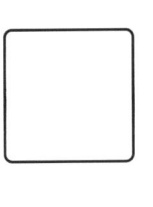

34.5 Multiplication Story Problems

Name: _____   Date: _____

Write and Solve

Use the picture or array to find the important numbers. Write them on the lines. Solve the problem and write the answer in the box.

There are ___ groups of ___ dice on the floor.
How many dice in total do we need to put away?

2 + 2 = ?
2 × 2 = ?

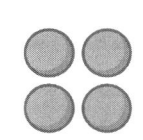

There are ___ groups of ___ dice on the floor.
How many dice in total do we need to put away?

3 + 3 + 3 = ?
3 × 3 = ?

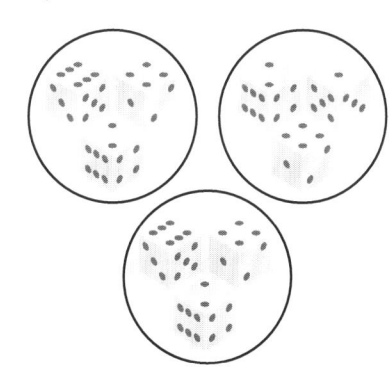

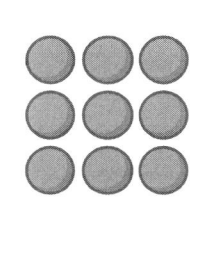

There are ___ groups of ___ pieces on the floor.
How many pieces in total do we need to put away?

6 + 6 = ?
2 × 6 = ?

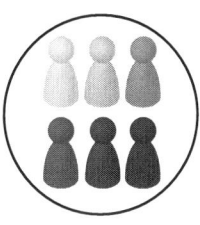

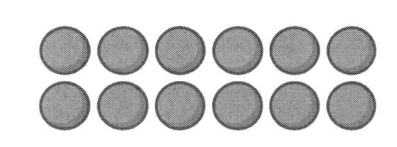

34.5 Multiplication Story Problems

Next page

There are __ piles of __ cards on the floor. How many cards in total do we need to put away?

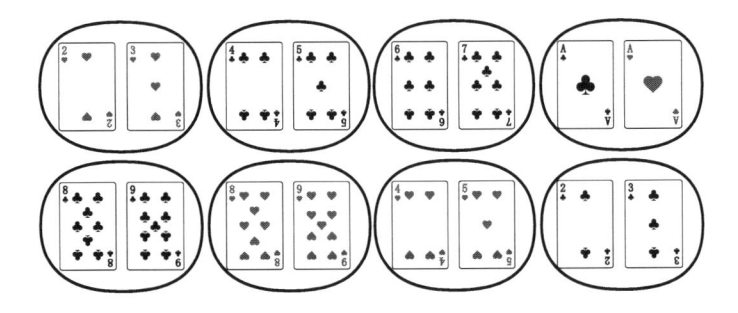

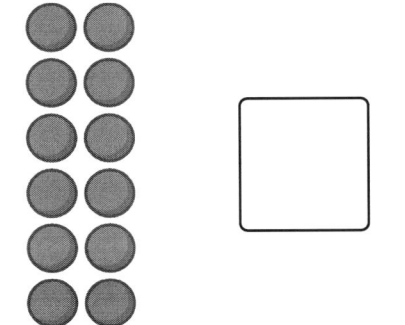

2+2+2+2+2+2+2+2 = ?
8 × 2 = ?

There are __ groups of __ dice on the floor. How many dice in total do we need to put away?

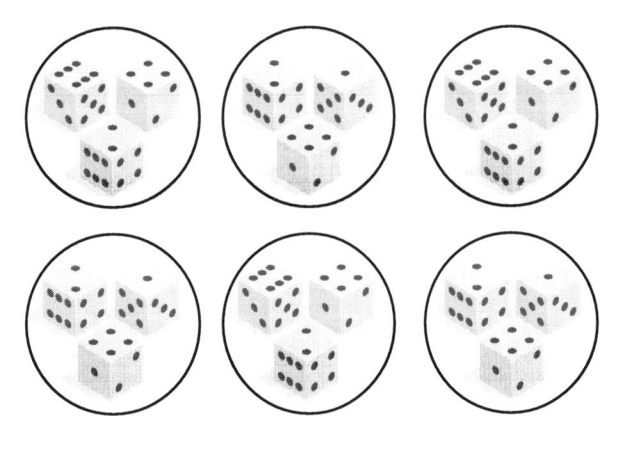

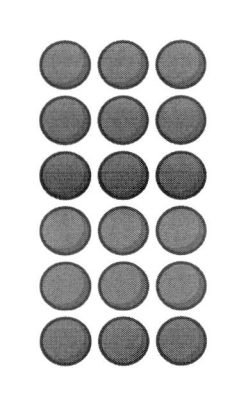

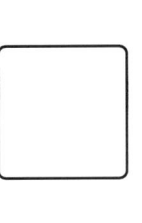

3+3+3+3+3+3 = ?
6 × 3 = ?

There are __ groups of __ pieces on the floor. How many pieces in total do we need to put away?

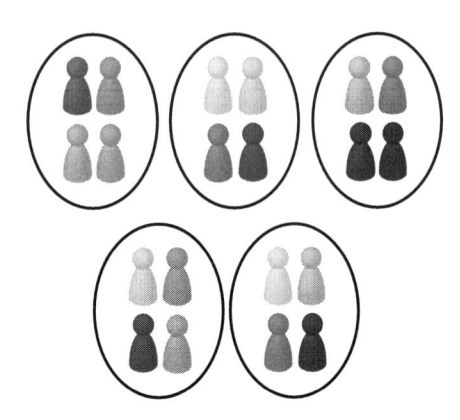

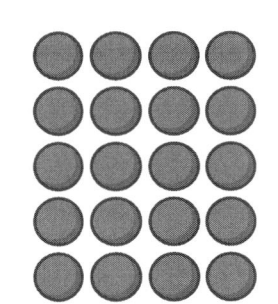

4 + 4 + 4 + 4 + 4 + 4 = ?
5 × 4 = ?

34.5 Multiplication Story Problems

Name: _____ Date: _____

Domino Multiplication

Write each multiplication sentence. Use your counters or a crayon to help you find the answer. Use the lesson to check your work!

___ X ___ = ___

35.1 Domino Multiplication

168

Next page

___ × ___ = ___

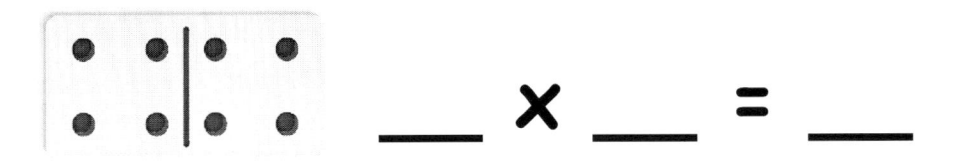

169   35.1 Domino Multiplication

Name: _____ Date: _____

Domino Multiplication

Use the domino to write the multiplication sentence. Then, use the strategy to find the answer. Write the answer in the box.

Example:

<u>5</u> × <u>2</u> = [10]

___ × ___ = [ ]

___ × ___ = [ ]

35.1 Domino Multiplication

170

Next page

___ × ___ = ☐

___ × ___ = ☐

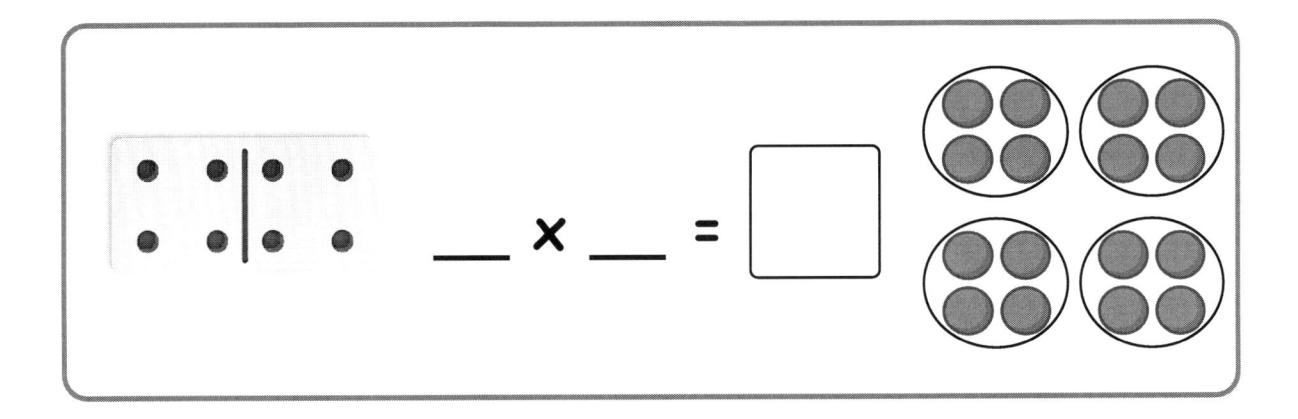

5, 10, 15, 20

Use your favorite strategy below to solve 3x5!

171 35.1 Domino Multiplication

Name: _____ Date: _____

Dice Multiplication

Use the dice to write the numbers before the = in each multiplication sentence. Pick any strategy to solve. Use the box for counters. Use the table for an array. Use the circles to make a multiplication picture. Use the blanks to skip count. Write the answer after the = .

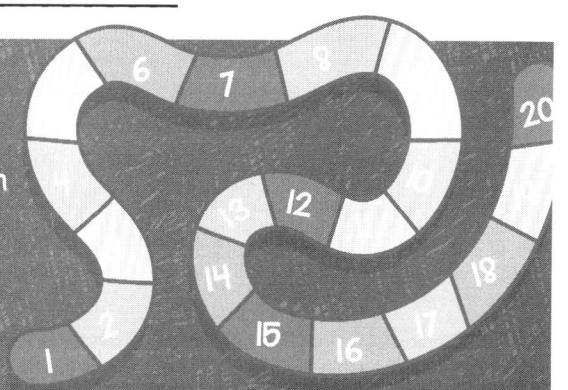

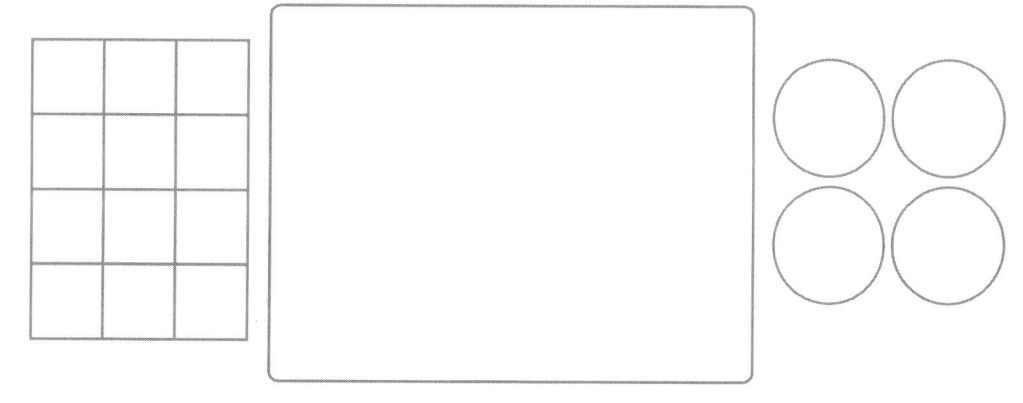

___ × ___ = ___

___, ___, ___, ___, ___

___ × ___ = ___

___, ___, ___, ___

35.2 Roll the Dice 172

Name: _____ Date: _____

Multiply to Win!

Fill in the box, blank array, circles, or lines to use a multiplication strategy. Find each answer. Move that number of spaces on the game board with a counter. Get to 41 to win!

Example:

$3 \times 4 = \underline{12}$ Move 12 spaces.

Counters go here!

Fill in the dots to make an array!

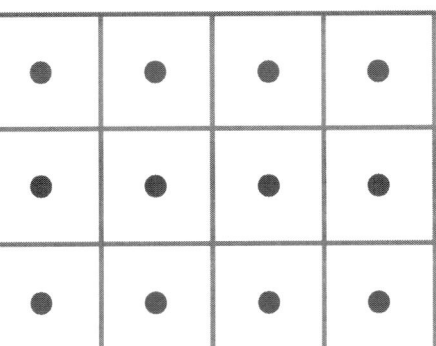

Fill in the dots to make a picture!

Put numbers on the lines to skip count!

___ , ___ , ___

173

35.2 Roll the Dice

Next page

5 × 1 = __

__, __, __, __, __

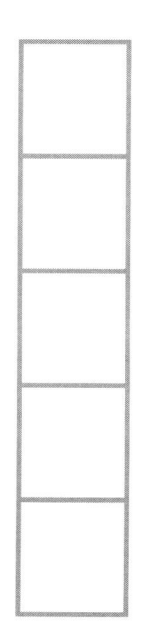

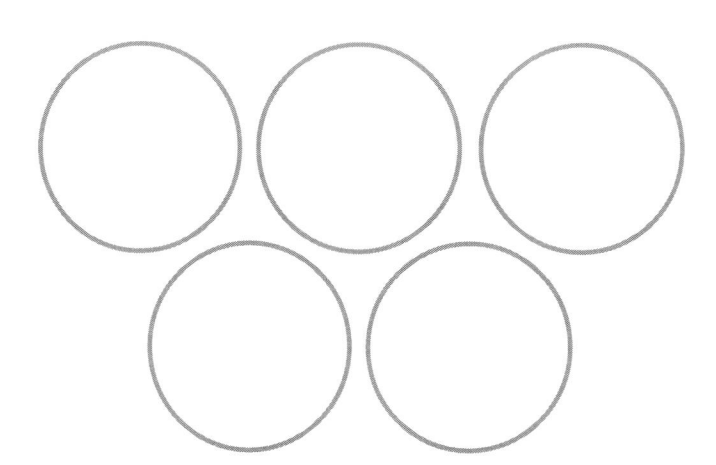

35.2 Roll the Dice

3 × 2 = ___

___ , ___ , ___

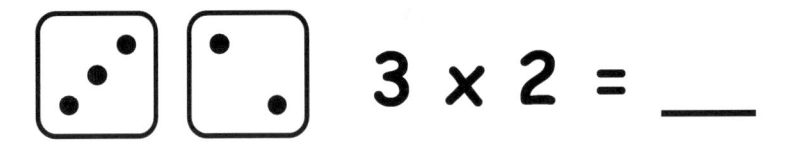

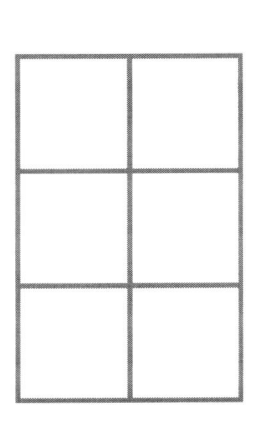

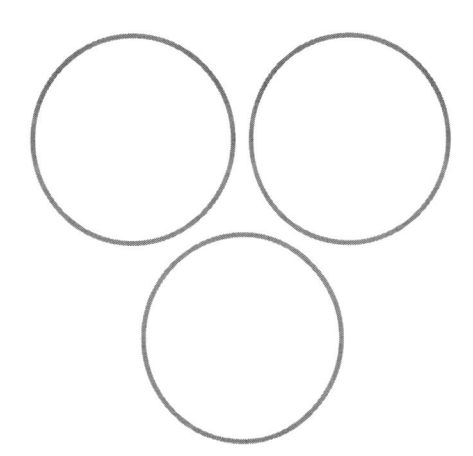

35.2 Roll the Dice

4 × 3 = ___

___ , ___ , ___ , ___

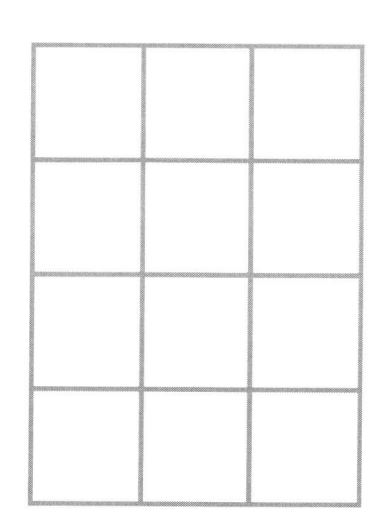

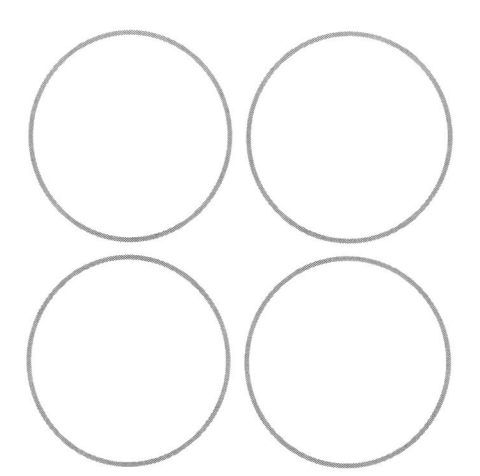

35.2 Roll the Dice

6 × 3 = ___

___, ___, ___, ___, ___

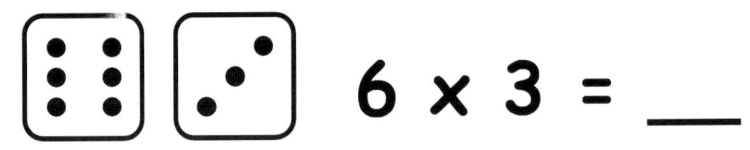

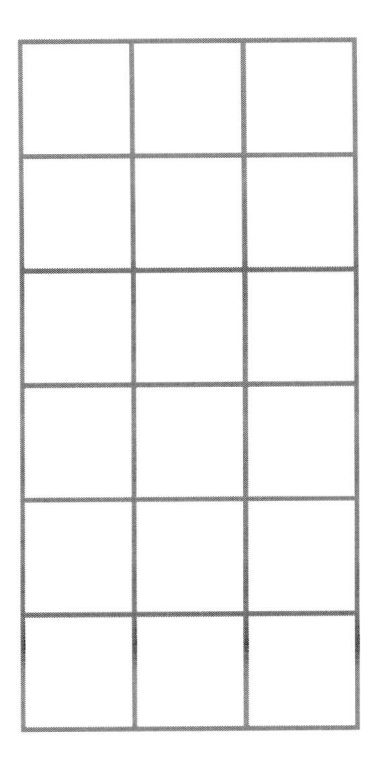

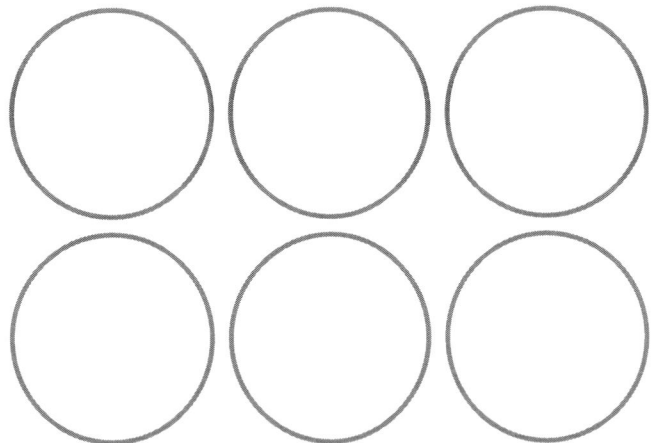

177

35.2 Roll the Dice

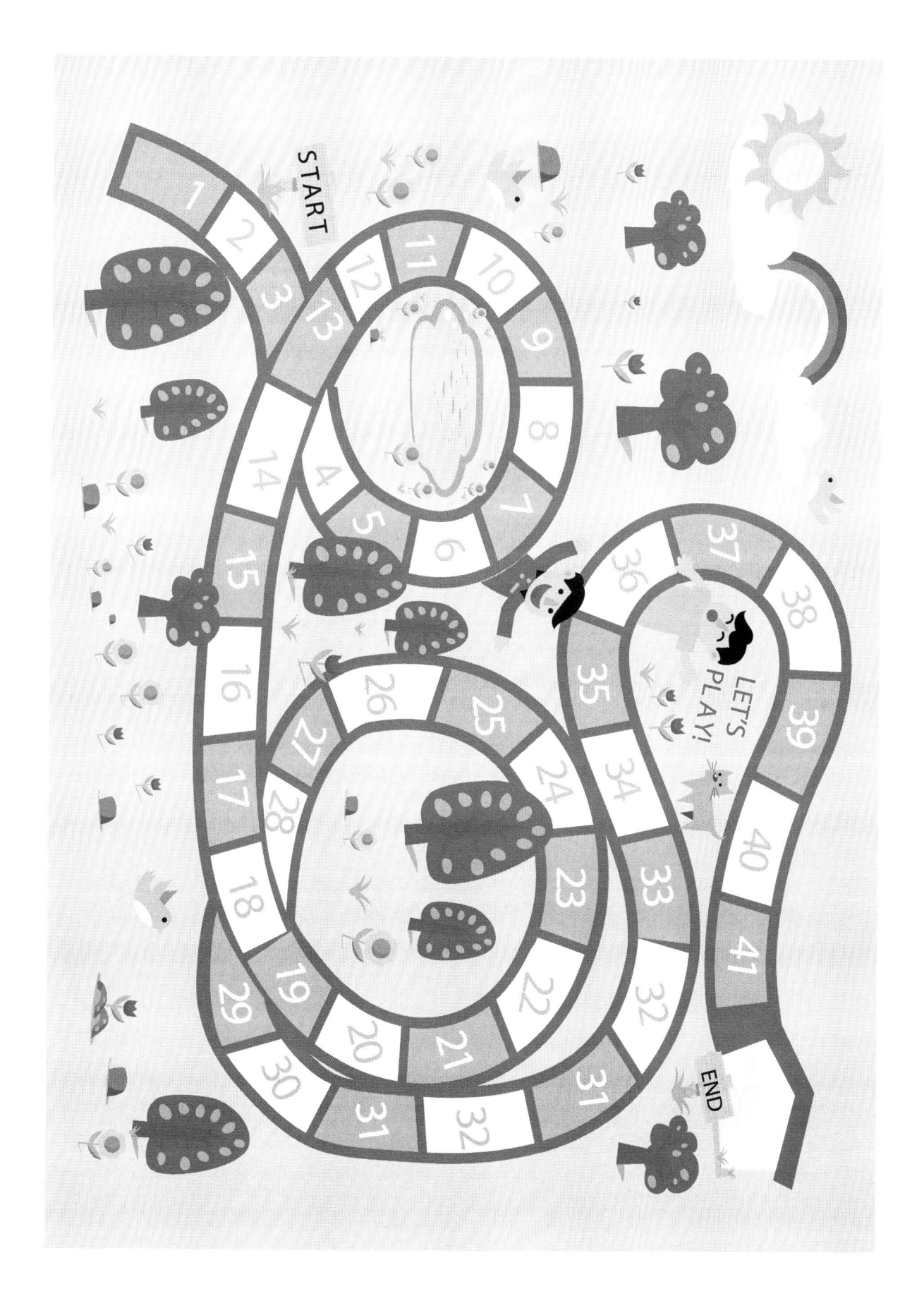

35.2 Roll the Dice

Name: _____ Date: _____

Multiplication Strategies

Use this sheet to help you choose a strategy to solve. Look at the examples to help you. Put your work in the boxes for the strategies you use.

Examples

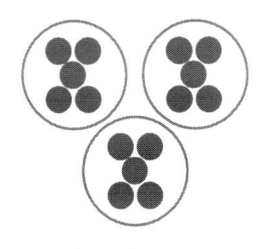

Counters   Array   Multiplication Picture   5, 10, 15   Skip Counting

Counters	Array

Multiplication Picture	Skip Counting

35.2 Roll the Dice

Name: _____ Date: _____

Flower Multiplication

Can you fill in the missing numbers in the multiplication flowers? Use any strategy to help you multiply!

Example:

1.

35.3 Flower Power

180

Next page

2.

3.

4.

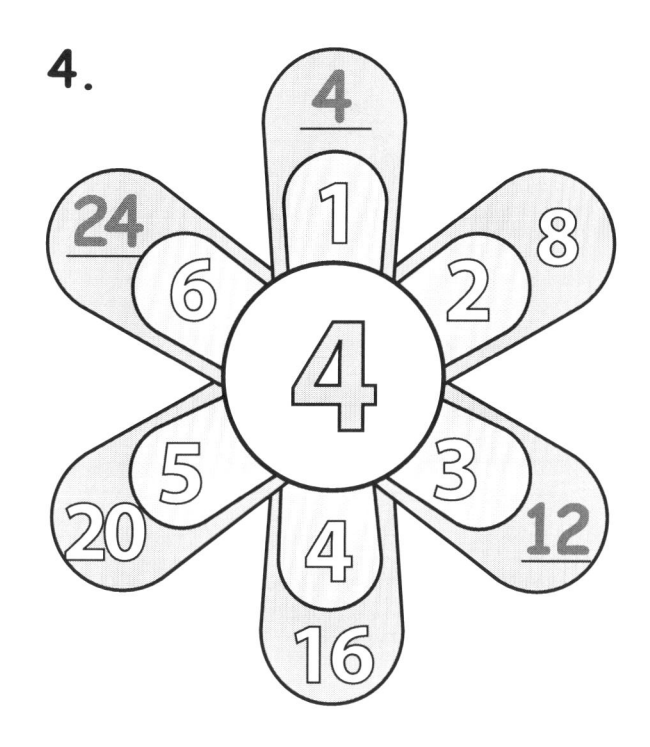

Fill out the multiplication flower. Write your answer on the line of each multiplication fact!

Multiply by 5
5 × 1 = __
5 × 2 = __
5 × 3 = __
5 × 4 = __
5 × 5 = __

35.3 Flower Power

Name: _____ Date: _____

Find 5 in a Row!

Multiply to find the products. Write each product on the line. Then, circle the product on the board until you get bingo.

4 × 4 = ___

2 × 10 = ___

6 × 3 = ___

1 × 19 = ___

17 × 1 = ___

8 × 3 = ___

BINGO

1	2	3	4	5
6	7	8	9	10
11	12	13	14	15
16	17	18	19	20
21	22	23	24	25

35.4 Multiplication Bingo

Name: _____ Date: _____

Build Fluency!

Find the product for each multiplication sentence. Write it on the line. Use a phone or your computer to time yourself! Write the time in minutes and seconds in the box. Have an adult check your work when you are done!

Minutes: ___   Seconds: ___

5 x 1 = ___   4 x 2 = ___

3 x 3 = ___   2 x 5 = ___

3 x 4 = ___   5 x 3 = ___

8 x 2 = ___   4 x 5 = ___

Let's try these facts again! The goal is to get the products in a shorter time. Time yourself and write the products on the lines.

Minutes: ___   Seconds: ___

3 x 3 = ___   5 x 3 = ___

5 x 1 = ___   3 x 4 = ___

4 x 2 = ___   2 x 5 = ___

4 x 5 = ___   8 x 2 = ___

35.5 Math Facts

Name: _____ Date: _____

Make Arrays

Put your items in rows and columns to make each array. Then draw a dot under each item. Write and solve the repeated addition and multiplication sentences!

4 by 3

___ + ___ + ___ + ___ = ___

___ x ___ = ___

5 by 5

___ + ___ + ___ + ___ + ___ = ___

___ x ___ = ___

185

36.1 Make Arrays

Name: _____ Date: _____

Make Arrays and Multiply!

How many rows and columns does each array need?
Draw dots to make the arrays.

Example: **2 by 2**

| 3 by 2 | 4 by 4 | 3 by 3 | 5 by 4 |

Use the arrays to fill in and solve the multiplication and repeated addition sentences.

Example:

$\underline{3} + \underline{3} = \underline{6}$

$\underline{2} \times \underline{3} = \underline{6}$

__ + __ + __ + __ = __

__ × __ = __

36.1 Make Arrays

186

Next page

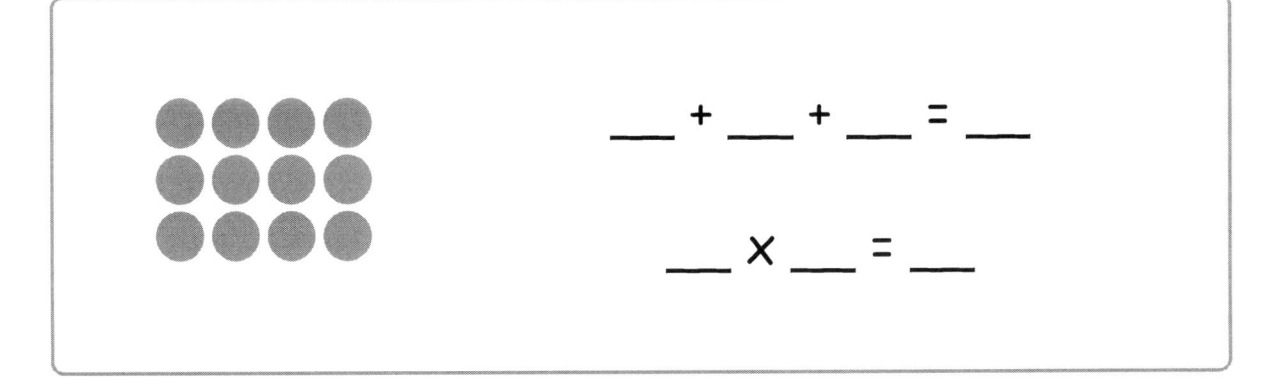

___ + ___ + ___ = ___

___ × ___ = ___

___ + ___ + ___ + ___ + ___ = ___

___ × ___ = ___

___ + ___ + ___ + ___ + ___ = ___

___ × ___ = ___

187

36.1 Make Arrays

Name: _____ Date: _____

Fill in the Houses

Use the multiplication and division sentences to complete the triangle. Then solve each multiplication and division sentence.

Example:

[6]
[2] [3]

2 × 3 = 6
3 × 2 = 6
6 / 2 = 3
6 / 3 = 2

3 × 3 = ___
3 × 3 = ___
9 / 3 = ___
9 / 3 = ___

9 × 2 = ___
2 × 9 = ___
18 / 9 = ___
18 / 2 = ___

5 × 4 = ___
4 × 5 = ___
20 / 5 = ___
20 / 4 = ___

8 × 3 = ___
3 × 8 = ___
24 / 8 = ___
24 / 3 = ___

36.2 Multiplication Fact Families

Name: _____ Date: _____

Array City

Draw an array. Then, use the array to complete the repeated addition or multiplication sentence. Find the answer and write it on both lines.

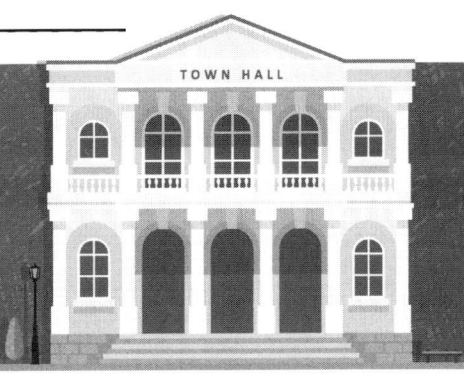

Example: 2 by 6

6 + 6 = 12

2 × 6 = 12

2 by 7

__ + __ = __

2 × 7 = __

4 by 4

4 + 4 + 4 + 4 = __

__ × __ = __

6 by 3

__ + __ + __ + __ + __ + __ = __

6 × 3 = __

4 by 5

5 + 5 + 5 + 5 = __

__ × __ = __

189

36.3 Array City

Name: _____ Date: _____

Multiplication Word Problems

Read each word problem. Solve the multiplication sentence for each problem.

Example: Ava drew 4 rows of 3 hearts. How many hearts did she draw in all? $\underline{4} \times \underline{3} = \underline{12}$

Liam drew 3 circles with 3 dots in each. How many dots did he draw in all?
$\underline{3} \times \underline{3} = \underline{}$

Sophia drew 2 groups of 5 hearts. How many hearts did she draw in total?
$\underline{2} \times \underline{5} = \underline{}$

Mia drew 3 rows of 4 smiley faces. How many smiley faces did she draw in total?
$\underline{3} \times \underline{4} = \underline{}$

Noah drew 5 boxes with 3 stars in each. How many stars did he draw in all?
$\underline{5} \times \underline{3} = \underline{}$

Riley drew 4 circles with 4 butterflies in each circle. How many butterflies did she draw in all?
$\underline{4} \times \underline{4} = \underline{}$

Caleb drew 9 rows of 2 flowers. How many flowers did he draw in total?
$\underline{9} \times \underline{2} = \underline{}$

Challenge: Which multiplication sentence goes with this problem? Circle it. Then find the answer!

Aaliyah drew 10 rows of 2 hearts. How many hearts did she draw in all?

$\underline{2} \times \underline{9} = \underline{}$ $\underline{10} \times \underline{2} = \underline{}$ $\underline{5} \times \underline{4} = \underline{}$

36.4 Word Problems

Name: _____ Date: _____

Solve with Seeds!

Read each problem. Then, write and solve each multiplication sentence. Use the listed color to color in the same number of seeds as the product.

Example:

Aria has 2 bags with 2 seeds in each bag. How many seeds does she have in all?

(Color in 4 seeds blue.)

$2 \times 2 = 4$ **BLUE**

---

1. Aria has 3 bags with 3 seeds in each bag. How many seeds does she have in all?

   ☐ × ☐ = ☐ **RED**

---

2. Aria has 2 bags with 6 seeds per bag. How many seeds does she have in total?

   ☐ × ☐ = ☐ **PURPLE**

---

3. Aria has 7 bags of 2 seeds. How many total seeds does she have?

   ☐ × ☐ = ☐ **ORANGE**

---

4. Aria has 5 bags with 5 seeds in each bag. How many seeds does she have in all?

   ☐ × ☐ = ☐ **PINK**

36.5 Write to Solve

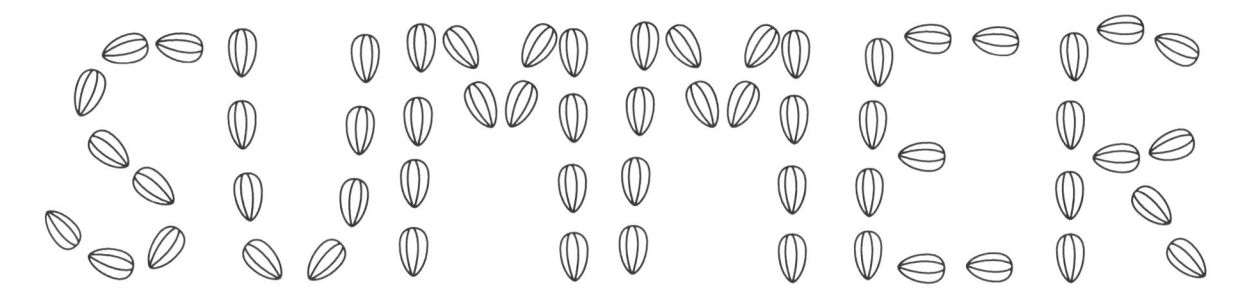

Have a GREAT SUMMER

Cutout Worksheets

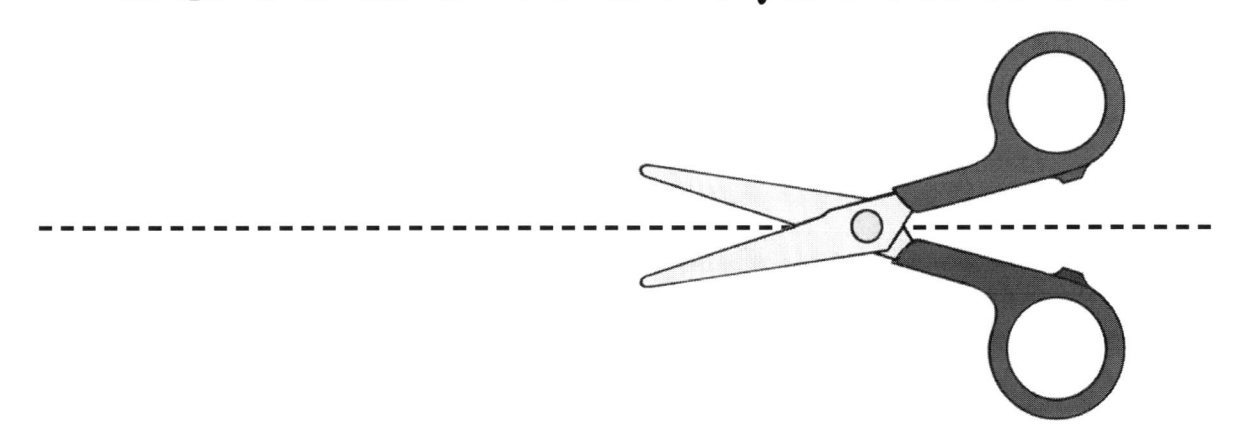

Name: _____ Date: _____

Problem Solve: Read and Interpret Data

Cut out the months. Then glue them to answer each question about the rainfall in Mumbai.

This graph shows us the amount of rainfall in Mumbai, India.

Average Rainfall in Mumbai

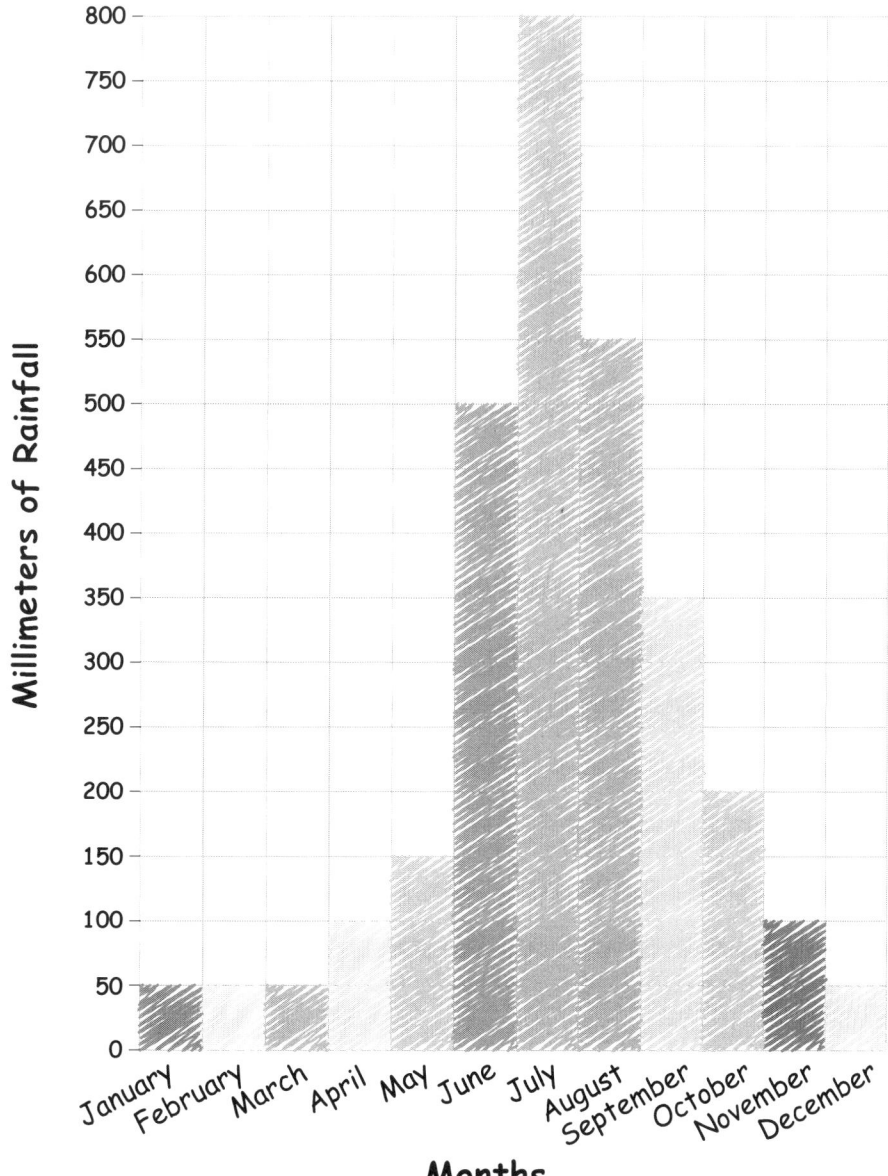

(Bar graph showing Millimeters of Rainfall by Months: January ~50, February ~0, March ~50, April ~0, May ~150, June ~500, July ~800, August ~550, September ~350, October ~200, November ~100, December ~50)

20.4 Problem Solve: Read and Interpret Data

194

Next page

1. In which months did it rain 50 millimeters?

2. Which month had the highest amount of rainfall?

3. Which months rained more than 300 millimeters but less than 600 millimeters?

4. In which month did it rain 200 millimeters?

5. In which months did it rain 100 millimeters?

6. In which month did it rain 150 millimeters?

January	February	March
April	May	June
July	August	September
October	November	December

20.4 Problem Solve: Read and Interpret Data

Name: _____ Date: _____

Place-Value Chart
Use this paper with your number cards to find the sum.

10   100   1

Hundreds	Tens	Ones

21.2 Break Apart 3-Digit Numbers to Add (Without Regrouping)

Name: _____ Date: _____

Number Cards

Cut out these cards and use them in the place-value chart.

0	1	2	3	4
5	6	7	8	9
0	1	2	3	4
5	6	7	8	9

21.2 Break Apart 3-Digit Numbers to Add (Without Regrouping) 200

Name: _____ Date: _____

Place-Value Chart

Use this paper with your number cards to find the sum.

Hundreds	Tens	Ones

21.3 Break Apart 3-Digit Numbers to Add (With Regrouping)

Name: _____ Date: _____

Number Cards

Cut out these cards and use them in the place-value chart.

0	1	2	3	4
5	6	7	8	9
0	1	2	3	4
5	6	7	8	9

21.3 Break Apart 3-Digit Numbers to Add (With Regrouping)

Name: _____ Date: _____

Place-Value Chart

Use this paper with your number cards to find the sum.

Hundreds	Tens	Ones

22.2 Break Apart 3-Digit Numbers to Subtract (Without Regrouping)

Name: _____ Date: _____

Number Cards

Cut out these cards and use them in the place-value chart.

0	1	2	3	4
5	6	7	8	9
0	1	2	3	4
5	6	7	8	9

22.2 Break Apart 3-Digit Numbers to Subtract (Without Regrouping)

Name: _____ Date: _____

Add and Subtract Numbers up to 1,000

Cut out each addition and subtraction sentence. Find the sums and differences. Then, glue them in the chart below.

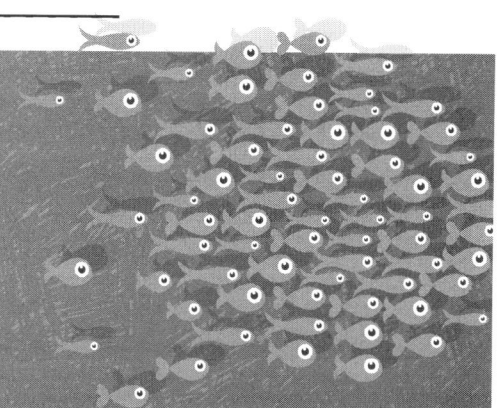

Hundreds

Does your answer have a **5 in the hundreds** place? Glue it here!

Tens

Does your answer have a **5 in the tens** place? Glue it here!

Ones

Does your answer have a **5 in the ones** place? Glue it here!

23.2 Add and Subtract Numbers up to 1000

```
 936        162        616
-413       + 97       +129
 ---        ---        ---


 329        956        273
+257       -806       -168
 ---        ---        ---
```

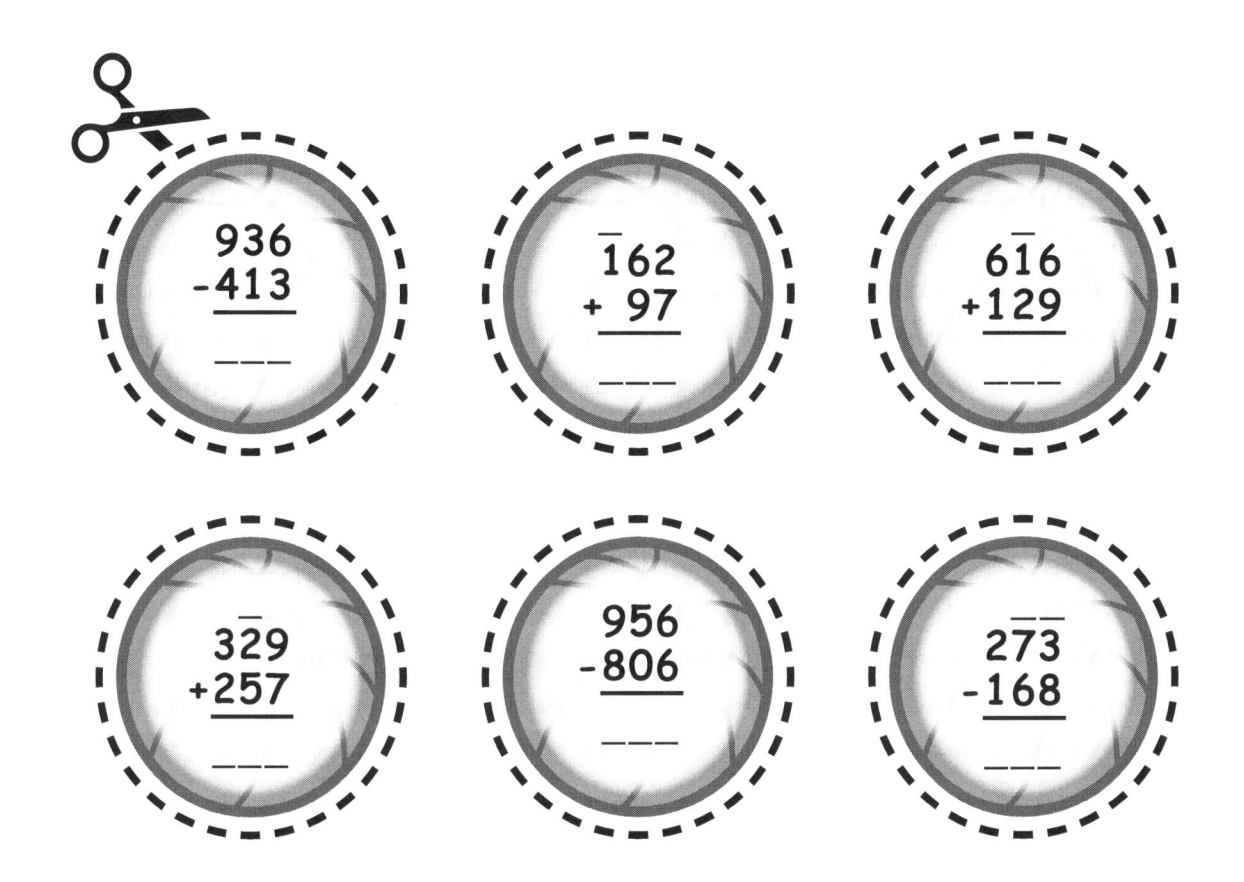

23.2 Add and Subtract Numbers up to 1000

What Operation?

What is the missing operation? Complete each number sentence using a plus sign (+) or a minus sign (-).

Number Sentence	Plus sign?	Minus sign?
91 ___ 46 = 45	91 + 46 ———	91 - 46 ——
56 ___ 23 = 79	56 + 23 ———	46 - 23 ——

✂ [+] [-]

23.3 What Operation?

Name: _____ Date: _____

Equation Paper

Make the numbers using your number cards.

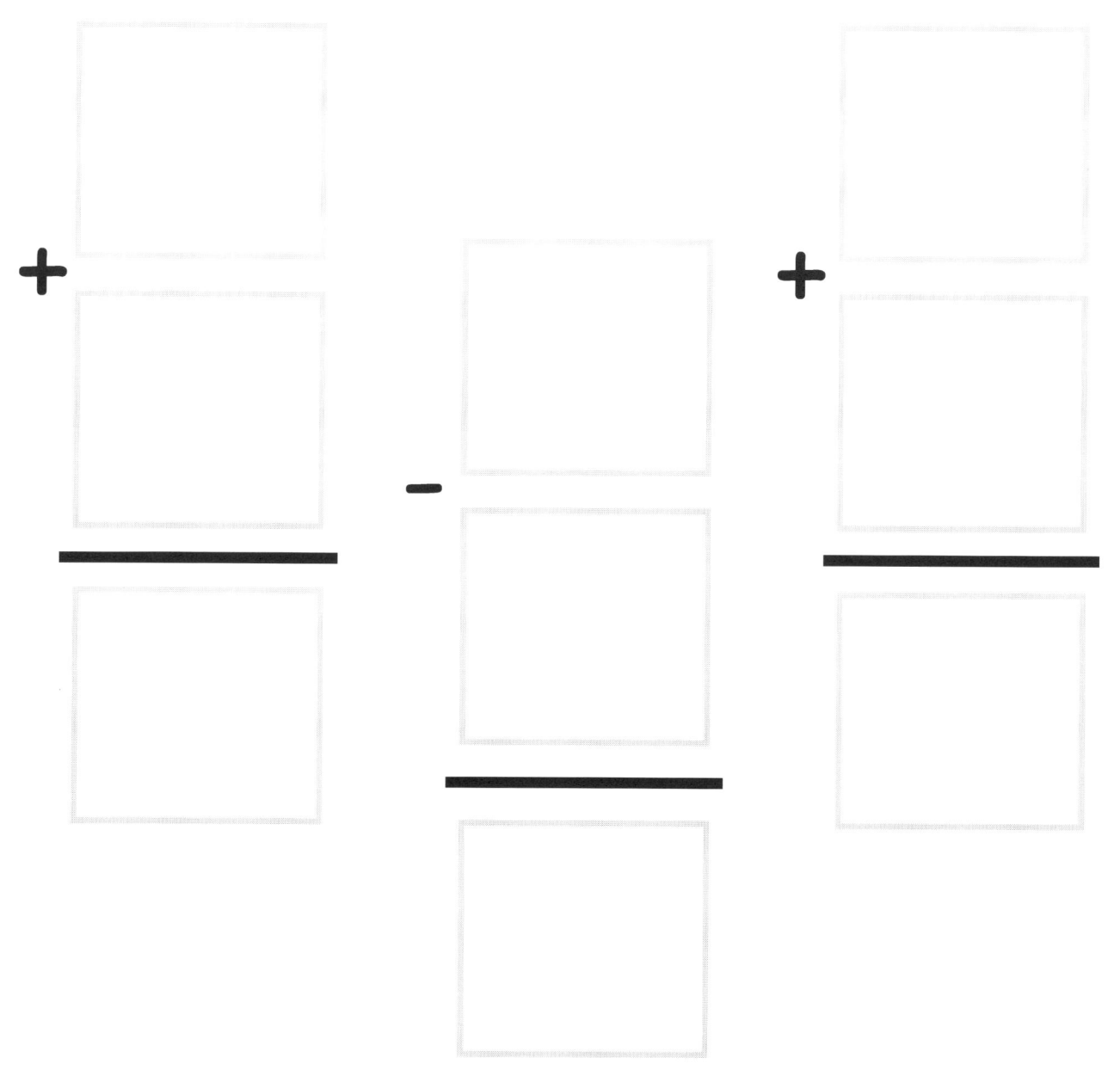

23.4 Ways to Make a Number

Name: _____ Date: _____

Number Cards

Cut out these cards and use them to make numbers on the equation paper.

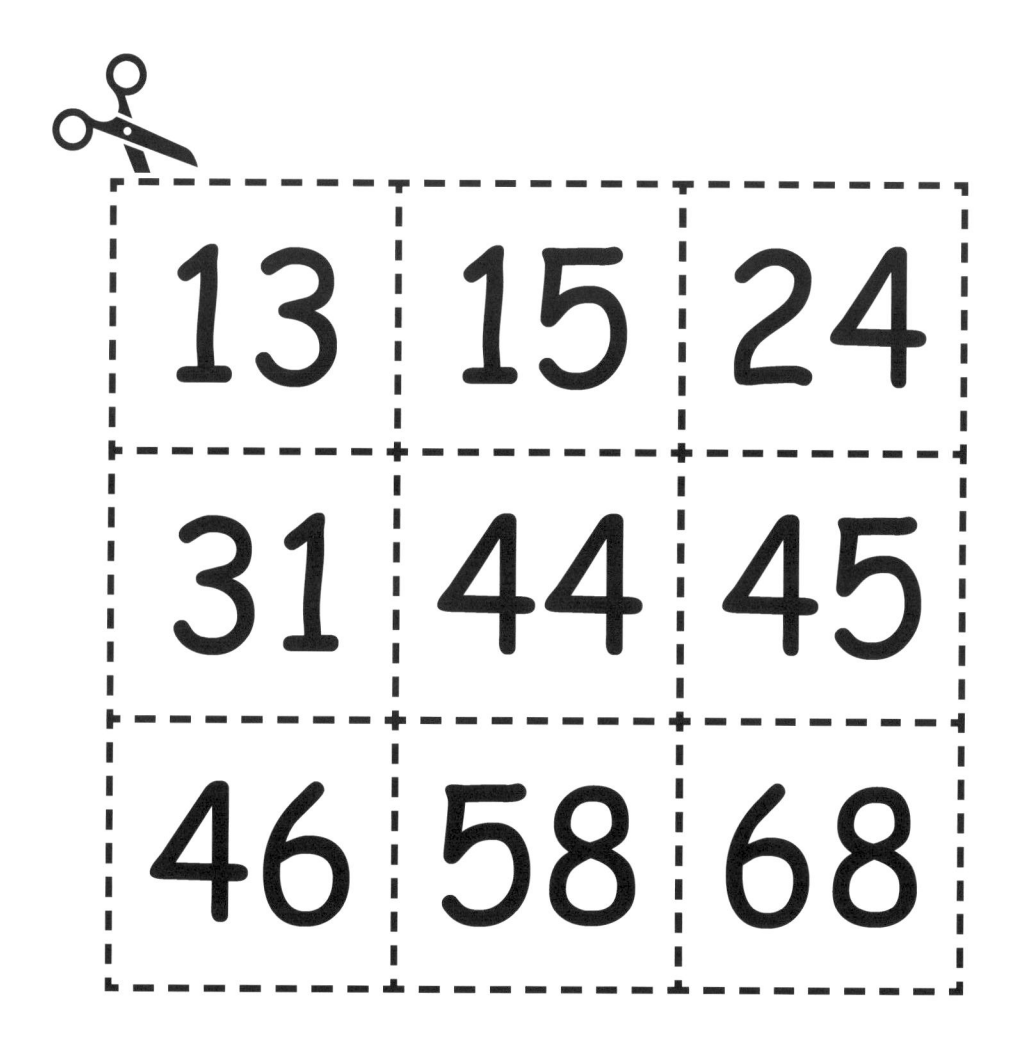

13	15	24
31	44	45
46	58	68

23.4 Ways to Make a Number

Name: _____ Date: _____

Word Problem Worksheet

Step 1: What are the numbers?

Cut out your number cards and use them to make an equation.

Step 2: What is the story?

I will write my word problem about _____.

What will happen in the word problem?

_____

_____

Step 3: What is the question?

I will ask this question at the end of my word problem:

_____

_____

24.5 Write Word Problems

Step 4: What is the key word?

This key word will tell people to add: _____.

Use the space below to write your word problem.

_____

_____

_____

_____

Name: _____ Date: _____

Number Cards

Cut out these cards and use them to make a word problem.

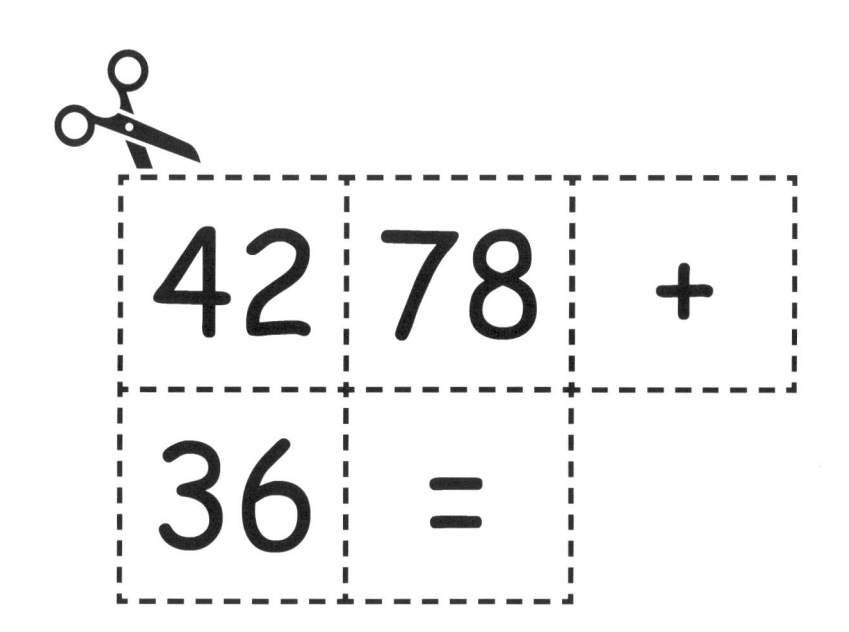

42	78	+
36	=	

24.5 Write Word Problems

Name: _____ Date: _____

Pizza Halves Sheet

1. Get a paper plate and fold it in half.
2. Draw a line down the fold.
3. Pick out two toppings. Cut them out.
4. Glue one topping on one ½ of the plate.
5. Glue the other topping on the other ½.
6. Write "½" on each side of the plate.

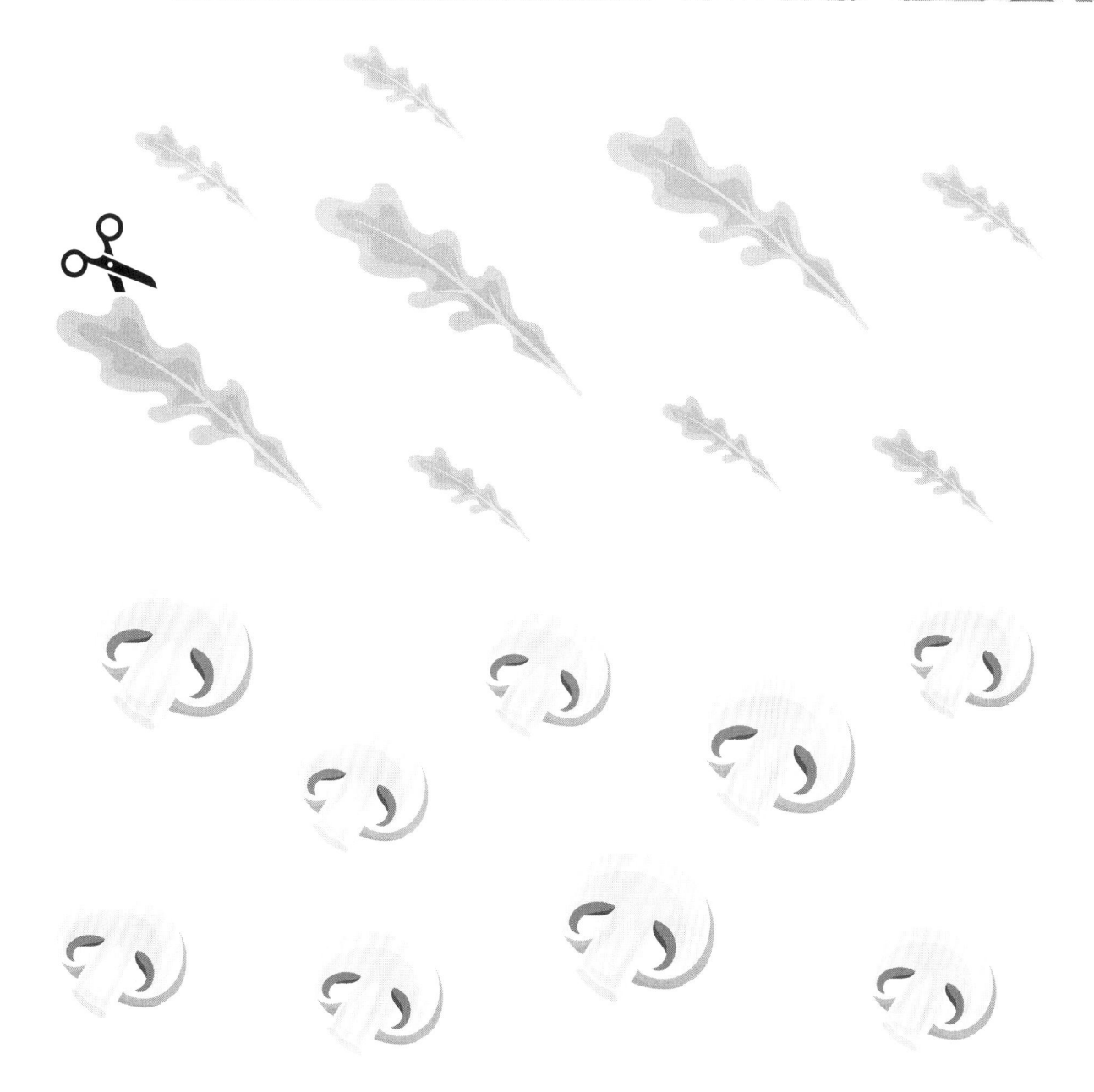

28.1 Fractions 1/2

224

Next page

28.1 Fractions 1/2

Name: _____ Date: _____

Blueprint Thirds

Follow each step to make the blueprint!
1. Color the blueprint with a blue crayon.
2. Cut out the blueprint.
3. Fold the right side of the paper to the lines on the left.
4. Open the paper and fold the left side of the paper to the lines on the right.
5. Draw a line down each fold.
6. Write $1/3$ on each third.

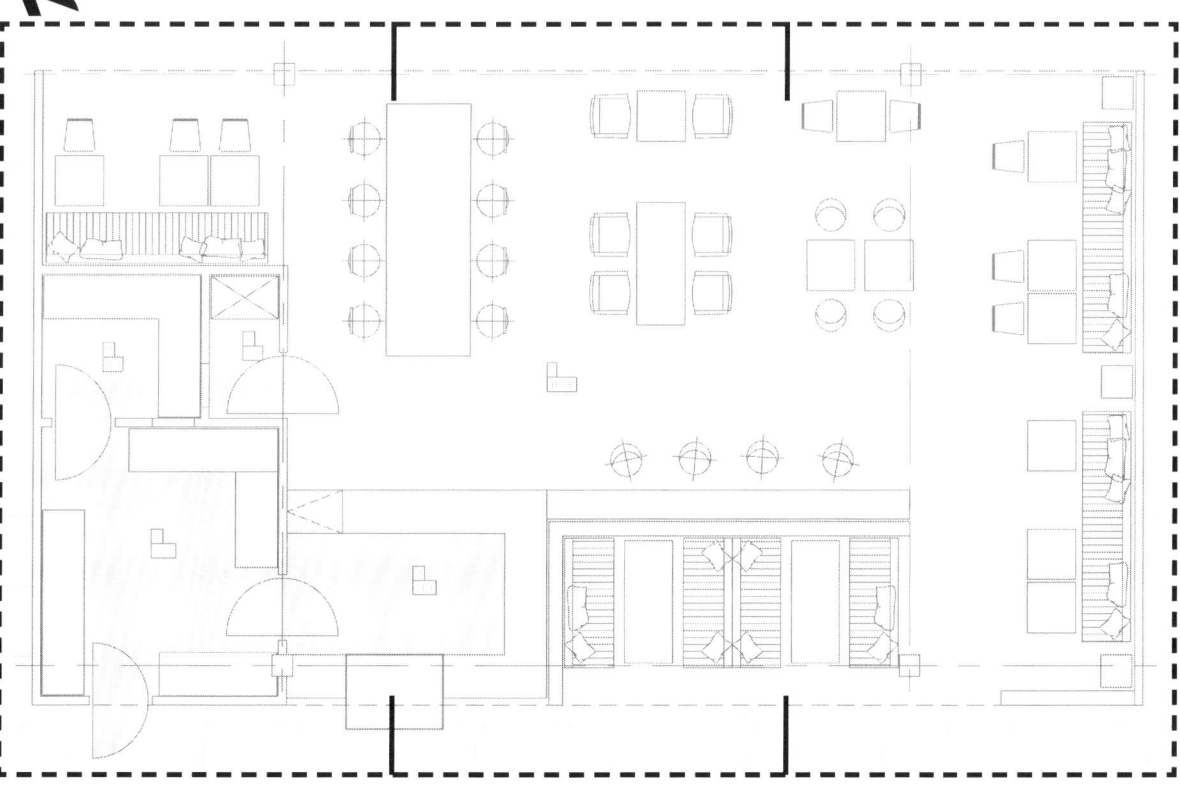

28.2 Fractions 1/3

Name: _____ Date: _____

Brick Fractions

1. Find a rectangular or square tissue box.
2. Place the box on the brick paper below. Trace the box.
3. Cut out the brick paper along the lines you traced. Glue the brick paper onto your tissue box.
4. Draw fourths on the brick paper with a marker.
5. Write ¼ on each fourth

28.3 Fractions 1/4

230

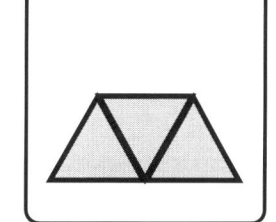

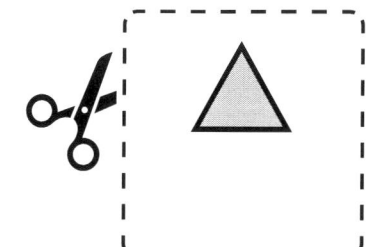

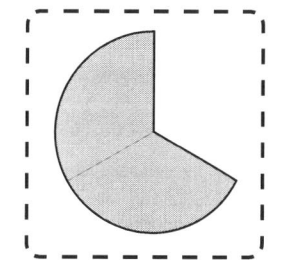

Name: _____ Date: _____

Adding Fractions

Can you find the parts to make whole shapes? Cut out and glue the pictures in the right boxes. Then draw the whole shapes in the box at the end of each sentence.

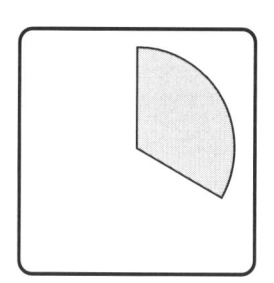

$\dfrac{1}{3}$ + $\dfrac{2}{3}$ = 1

$\dfrac{1}{4}$ + $\dfrac{3}{4}$ = 1

28.4 Add Fractions

Name: _____ Date: _____

A.M. and P.M.
Help Binx the Beagle decide during what part of the day you would do different activities. Cut out the activities and paste them under A.M. or P.M.

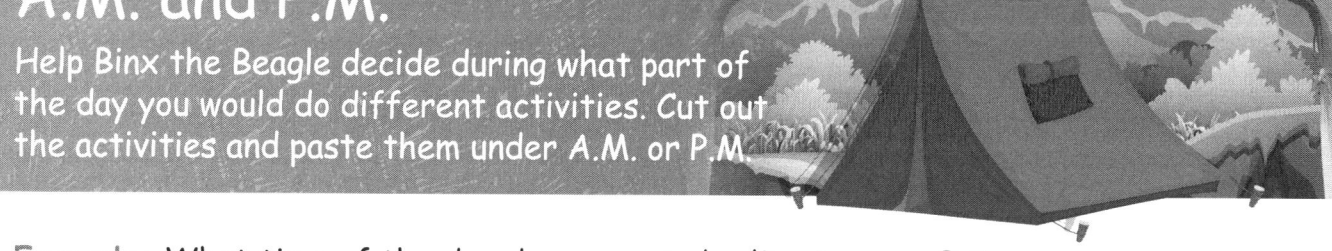

Example: What time of the day do you go to bed?   Answer: P.M.

What activities would you do during the A.M.?	What activities would you do during the P.M.?

30.1 A.M. and P.M.

234

Next page

Ride your bike after lunch.

Watch the sunrise.

Watch cartoons on Saturday morning!

Go fishing on a Sunday morning!

Walk to the school bus stop in the morning.

Go to the movies Friday night!

Sing songs around a campfire in the evening.

Walk your dog after school.

30.1 A.M. and P.M.

Name: _____ Date: _____

Cutout Clock for Problem Solving!
Cut out the clock and the clock hands. Attach the hands to the clock using a brad fastener.

30.3 Word Problems: Time

238

Pennies, Nickels, and Dimes

Count the value of the coins.
Write the total amount on the line.

Example

25 ¢

1. ___ ¢

2. ___ ¢

3. ___ ¢

4. ___ ¢

5. ___ ¢

31.1 Pennies, Nickels, and Dimes

240

Next page

Your Turn!

Cut the coins and paste them to show the correct total value.
Hint: Try using the largest coins first, and then see how much more you need.

Example:

1. Show 35¢ =

2. Show 10¢ =

3. Show 19¢ =

4. Show 33¢ =

31.1 Pennies, Nickels, and Dimes

Coin Cutouts

Use the following coin cutouts to count the value of coins in the lesson.

31.1 Pennies, Nickels, and Dimes

Name: _____ Date: _____

Ways to Show the Same Amount

Circle the answer that equals the **value** of the coins.

Example

(25¢)   50¢   75¢ $1

1.

25¢   50¢   75¢ $1

2.

25¢   50¢   75¢ $1

3.

25¢   50¢   75¢ $1

31.2 Quarters

4.

| 25¢ | 50¢ | 75¢ | $1 |

5.

| 25¢ | 50¢ | 75¢ | $1 |

6.

| 25¢ | 50¢ | 75¢ | $1 |

7.

| 25¢ | 50¢ | 75¢ | $1 |

245   31.2 Quarters

Coin Cutouts

Cut out the coins along the dotted lines. Use them to help you count the value of coins in the lesson.

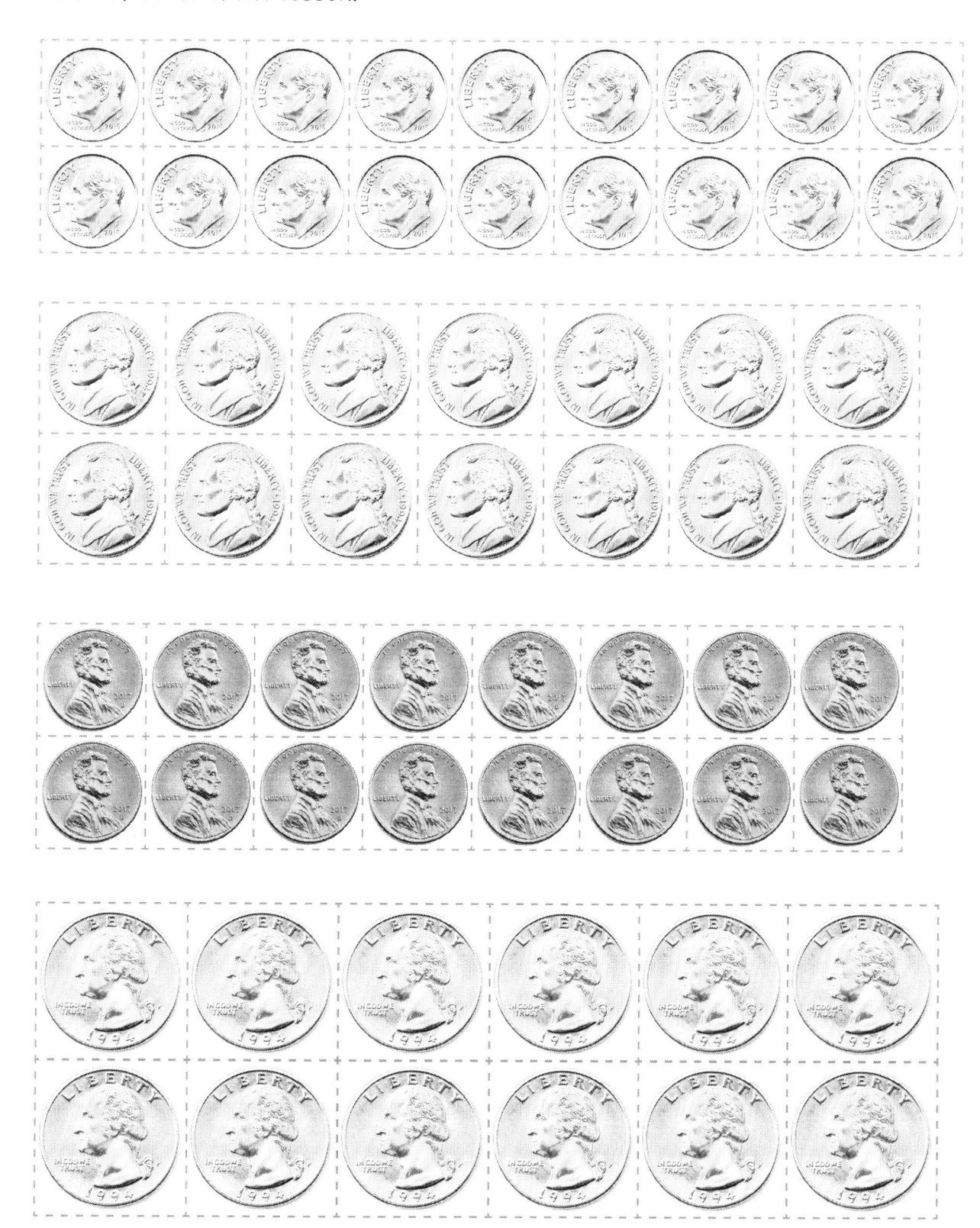

31.2 Quarters

Name: _____ Date: _____

Making Change to a Dollar

It costs a dollar to watch the Kite Festival. Cut out the coins and paste them in the squares to show four different ways to make a dollar.

Example

First Way

Second Way

Third Way

Fourth Way

31.3 Dollars

248

Next page

Coin Cutouts

Cut out the coins along the dotted lines. Use them to help you count the value of coins in the lesson.

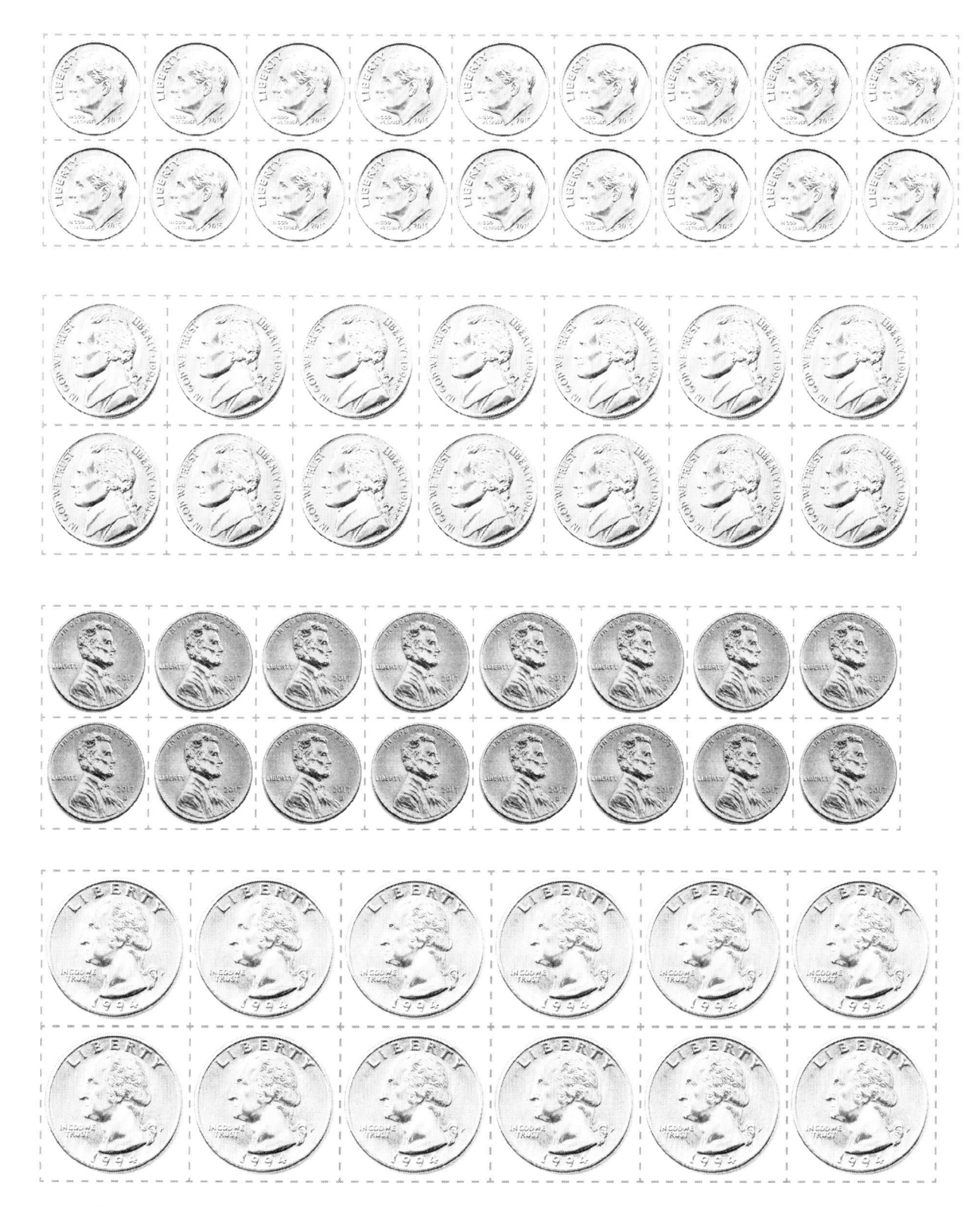

31.3 Dollars

250

Name: _____ Date: _____

Show Coin Combinations to Make Change

How many of each coin do you need to equal **70 cents**?
Fill in the blanks to show the coin amounts.
Paste the coins in the right column.

Example:

_1_ quarter
_4_ dimes
_1_ nickel

___ dimes

___ quarters
___ pennies

31.4 Count Coins

252

Next page

___ quarters
___ nickels

___ dimes
___ nickels

___ dimes
___ nickels
___ pennies

Coin Cutouts

Cut out the coins along the dotted lines. Use them to help you count the value of coins in the lesson.

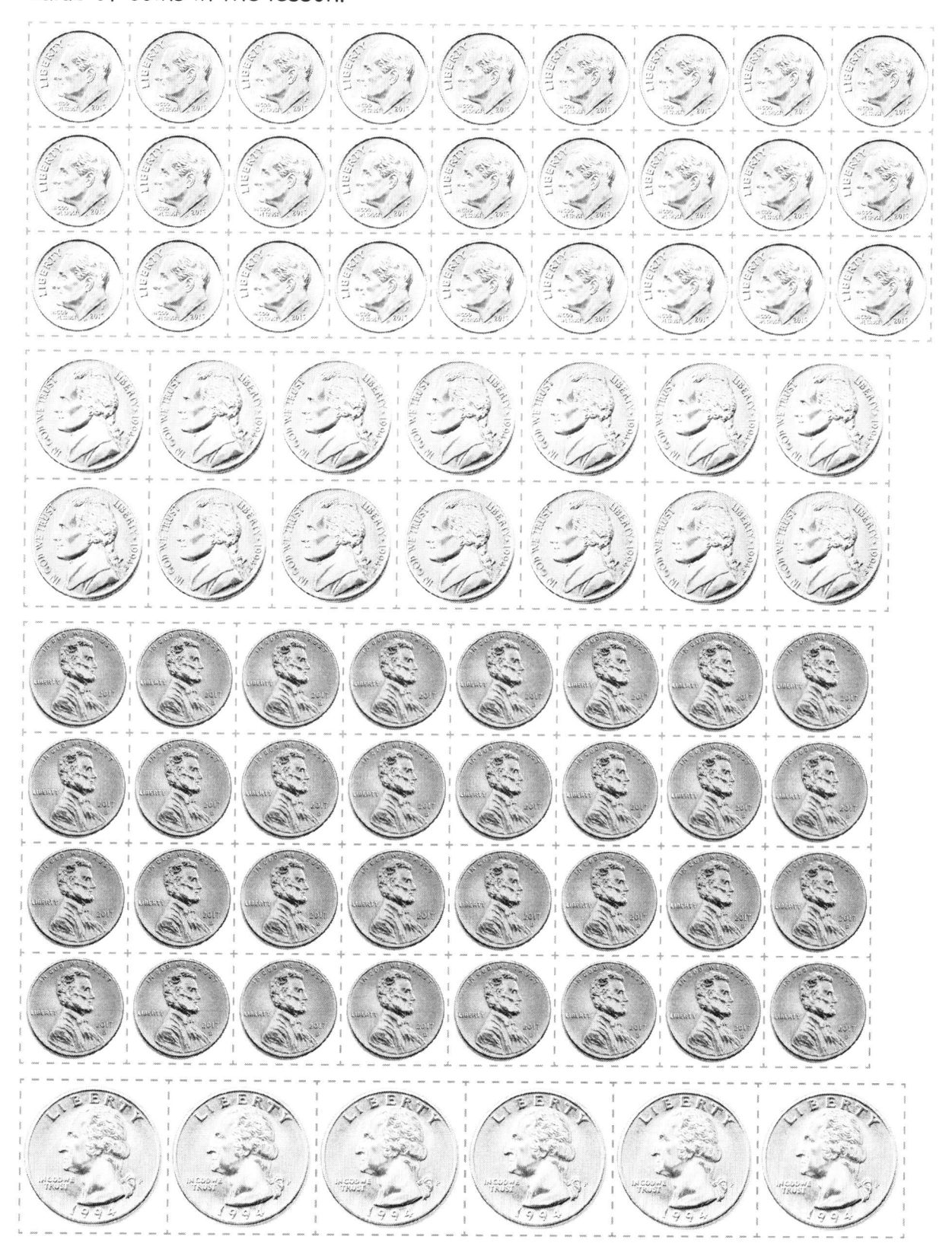

31.4 Count Coins

Name: _____ Date: _____

Solve Money Problems Using Money Symbols

Draw or use the coin cutouts to help you find the coin values to solve the problems.

Example:

Keegan has 5 nickels and 9 pennies. Does she have enough money to buy a pencil that costs 50¢?

Yes or (No)
Keegan has 34¢

Add - 5¢ + 5¢ + 5¢ + 5¢ + 5¢ + 1¢ + 1¢ + 1¢ + 1¢ + 1¢ + 1¢ + 1¢ + 1¢ + 1¢
       25¢   9¢

```
  25¢
+  9¢
-----
  34¢
```

Count up

5¢, 10¢, 15¢, 20¢, 25¢, 26¢, 27¢, 28¢, 29¢, 30¢, 31¢, 32¢, 33¢, 34¢

Tyler wants to buy a toy car. It costs 86¢. He has 3 quarters and 2 dimes. Does he have enough money to buy the toy car?

Yes or No
Tyler has ___ ¢

31.5 Problem Solving

256

Next page

Holly has 1 quarter, 3 dimes, and 3 nickels. She wants to buy some stickers that cost 75¢. Does Holly have enough money to buy the stickers?

Yes or No

Holly has ___ ¢

Juan needs a new pen. It costs $1.25. He has 6 quarters. Does he have enough money to buy the pen?

Yes or No

Juan has $ ___

Rhonda wants a new kite. It costs $1.50. She has $1 and 4 quarters. Does she have enough money to buy the kite?

Yes or No

Rhonda has $ ___

Coin Cutouts

Cut out the coins along the dotted lines. Use them to help you count the value of coins in the lesson.

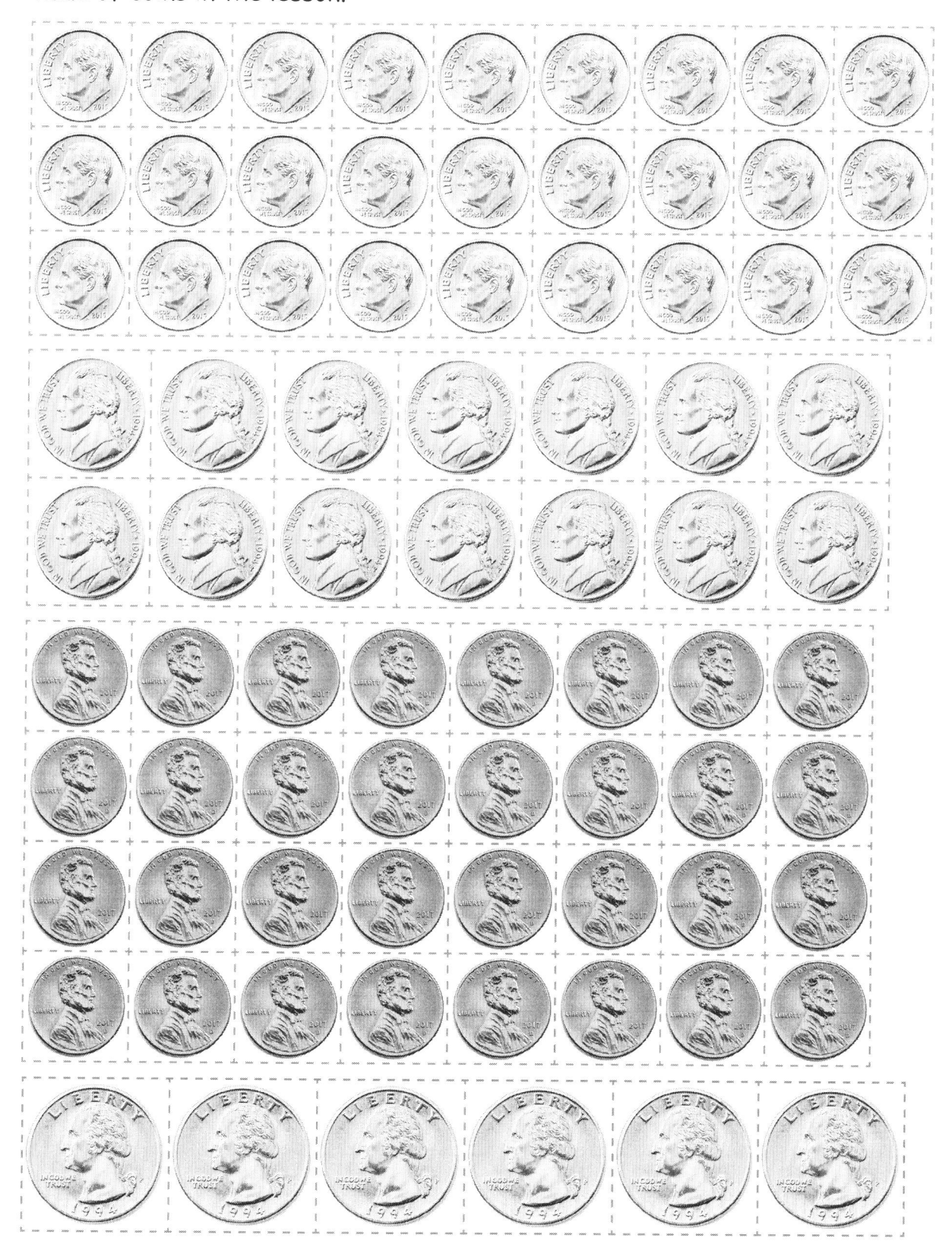

31.5 Problem Solving

Name: _____ Date: _____

Make and Analyze Picture Graphs

Bean the Robot loves hot dogs! He has gathered data from the hot dog food cart! Students ate different kinds of hot dogs. Let's gather the data and make a picture graph to show what they picked!

Complete the tally mark data chart and picture graph.

Hot Dog Favorites	Total Number of Students	Tally Marks
 Example: Hot Dogs	5	|||||
 Corn Dogs	10	
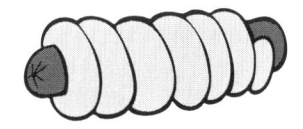 Bagel Dogs	6	
 Chili Dogs	8	
 Sausage Dogs	3	

32.3 Make and Analyze Picture Graphs

260

Next page

Hot Dog Favorites

Hot Dogs	Corn Dogs	Bagel Dogs	Chili Dogs	Sausage Dogs

32.3 Make and Analyze Picture Graphs

Let's analyze the data! Answer the following questions.

1. What is the title of the graph?

2. What are the top two favorite hot dogs?

3. Which hot dog is the least favorite?

4. Which hot dog was liked by 6 students?

5. How many students altogether ate hot dogs at the hot dog stand?

Cut and paste the Hot Dog Favorite tally mark data to make a picture graph!

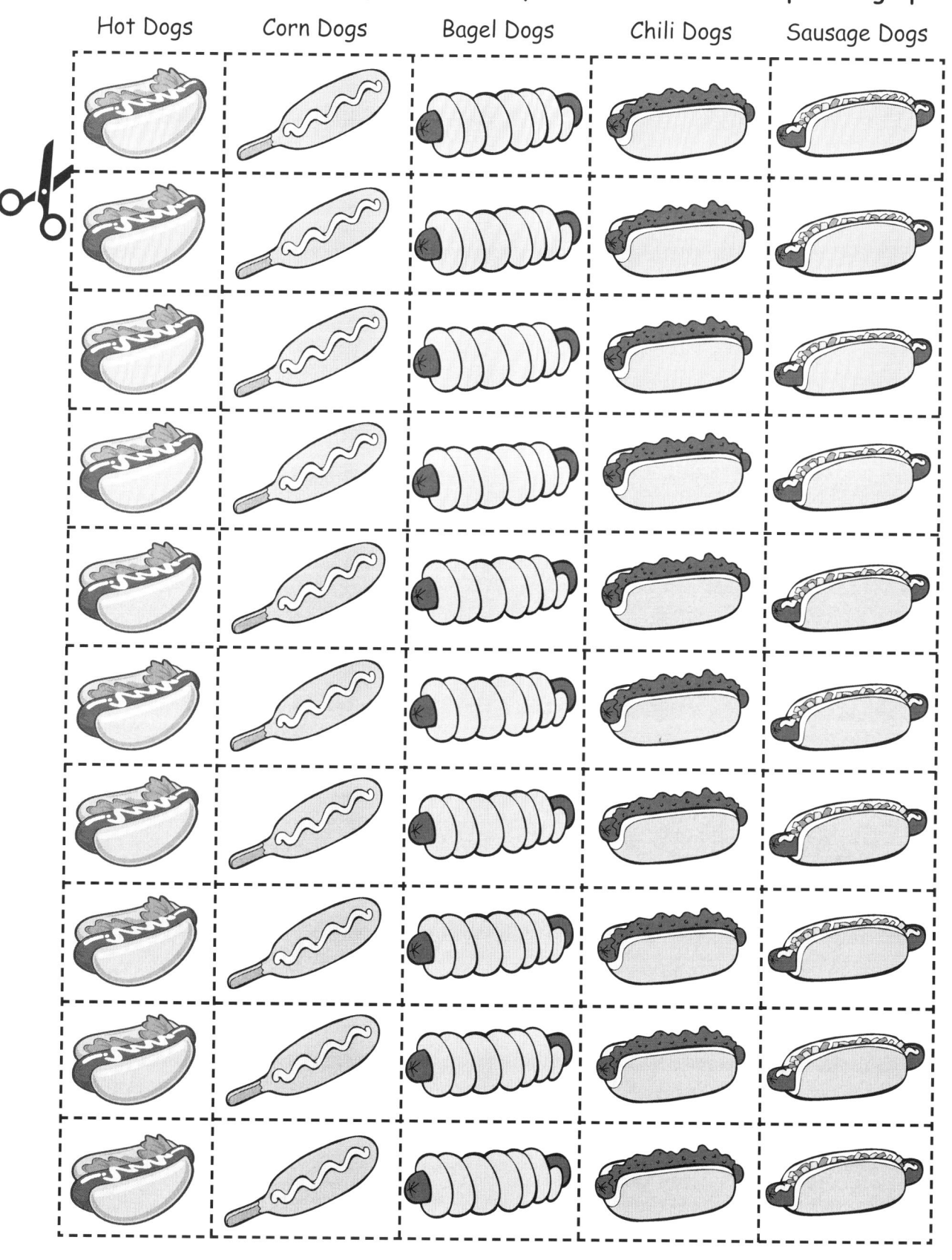

| Hot Dogs | Corn Dogs | Bagel Dogs | Chili Dogs | Sausage Dogs |

32.3 Make and Analyze Picture Graphs

264

Name: _____ Date: _____

Multiplication Matching

How many bumper cars are there? Cut out the multiplication pictures. Glue them in the boxes to match the multiplication and addition sentences.

4 x 1 = 4
1 + 1 + 1 + 1 = 4

3 x 5 = 15
5 + 5 + 5 = 15

6 x 2 = 12
2 + 2 + 2 + 2 + 2 + 2 = 12

33.5 Multiplication Matching

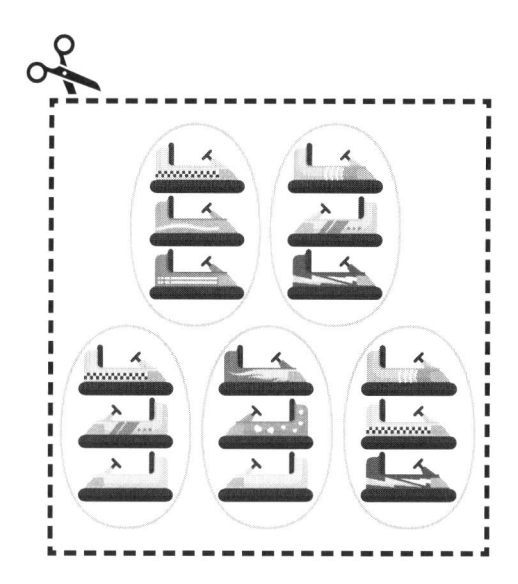

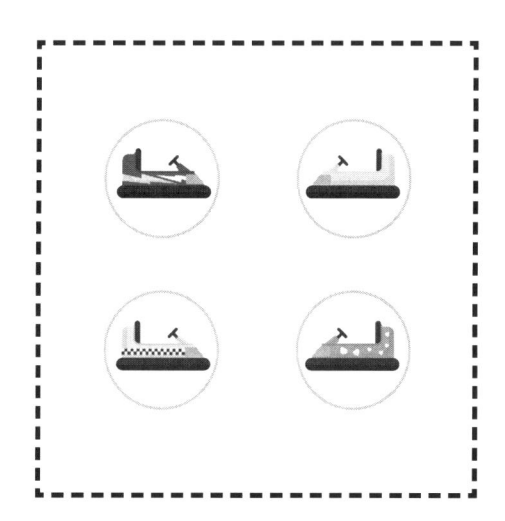

33.5 Multiplication Matching

268

Name: _____ Date: _____

Problem Solving

Cut out the arrays. Read each problem. Glue the correct array in each box. Then use the array and the repeated addition sentence to find the answer! Write the answer to each problem on the line.

We have 6 rows with 2 blocks in each row. How many blocks do we have in all?

2 + 2 + 2 + 2 + 2 + 2 = ?

6 x 2 = ?

_____

We have 4 rows of 5 blocks. How many blocks do we have in total?

5 + 5 + 5 + 5 = ?

4 x 5 = ?

_____

34.4 Problem Solving

270

Next page

34.4 Problem Solving

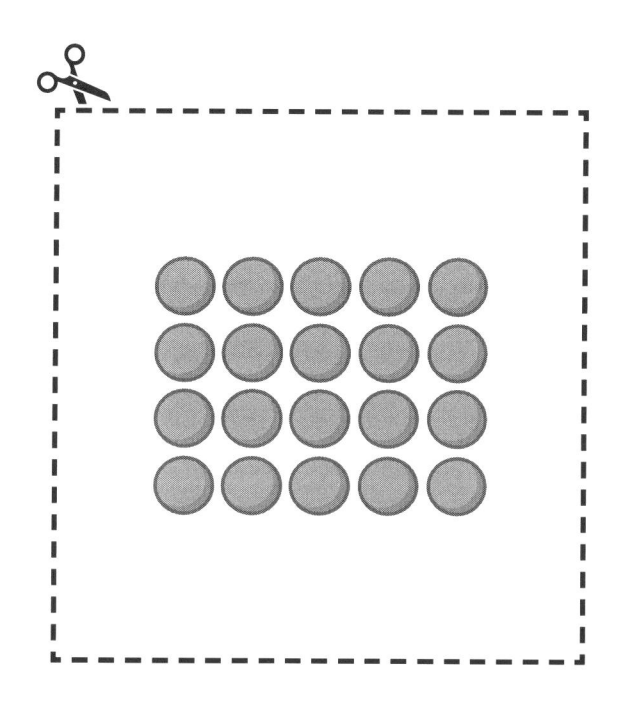

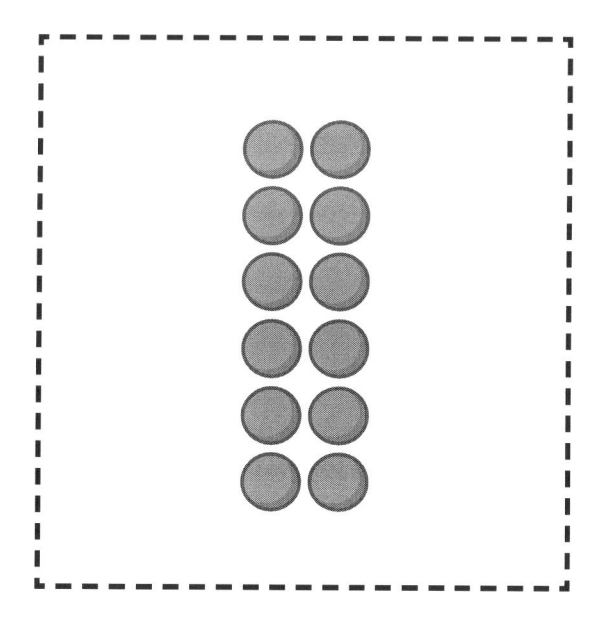

272

Name: _____ Date: _____

Multiplication Power

Use any strategy to find the correct answers. Cut out and glue the correct answers to the petals. Then write the answer on the line of each multiplication sentence.

Multiply by 3

3 x 1 = ___

3 x 2 = ___

3 x 3 = ___

3 x 4 = ___

3 x 5 = ___

Multiply by 4

4 x 1 = ___

4 x 2 = ___

4 x 3 = ___

4 x 4 = ___

4 x 5 = ___

| 3 | 4 | 6 | 8 | 9 | 12 | 12 | 15 | 16 | 20 |

35.3 Flower Power

Name: _____ Date: _____

Cover It All!

Let's play coverall! Cut out the multiplication sentences. Match them to the correct products to fill in the bingo board!

	2			
6		8		
	12	13		15
		18		
21			24	25

35.4 Multiplication Bingo

276

Next page

$1 \times 2 = ?$	$2 \times 3 = ?$	$5 \times 5 = ?$	$2 \times 9 = ?$	$4 \times 2 = ?$
$13 \times 1 = ?$	$5 \times 3 = ?$	$4 \times 6 = ?$	$3 \times 4 = ?$	$7 \times 3 = ?$

35.4 Multiplication Bingo

Name: _____ Date: _____

Fluency Flashcards

Let's practice some multiplication facts! Write the answer on the back of each flashcard. Use the lesson to check your work. You can cut the cards out and use them to build fluency!

4 × 2 =	1 × 7 =	4 × 2 =	11 × 1 =
6 × 2 =	4 × 4 =	3 × 6 =	1 × 19 =
	2 × 10 =	8 × 3 =	

35.5 Math Facts

Next page

35.5 Math Facts

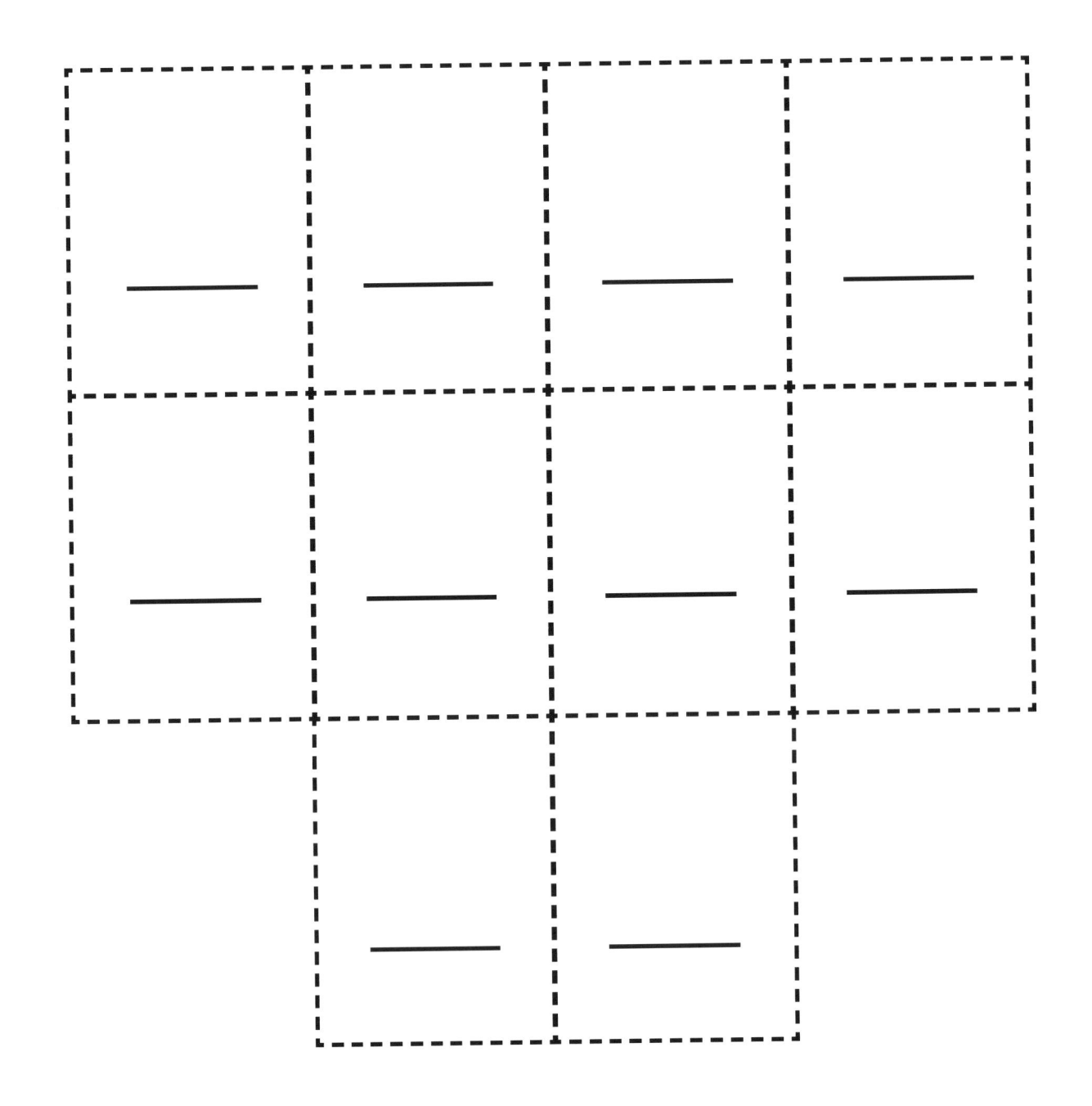

Name: _____ Date: _____

Fact Family Houses

Cut out the numbers and glue them in the triangles. Then use the numbers to fill in the sentences of the fact families!

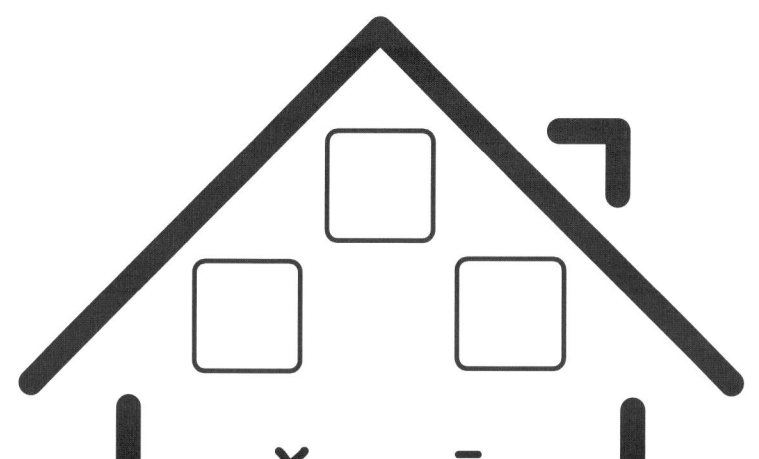

✂ [7] [2] [14]

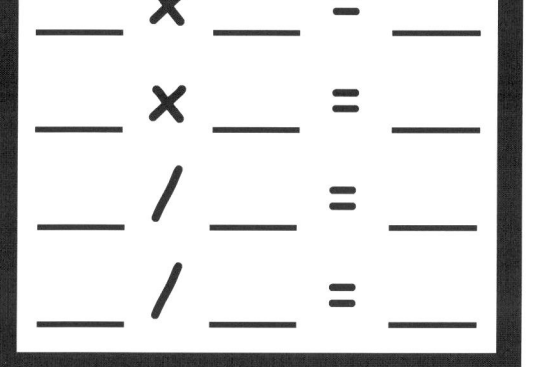

___ × ___ = ___
___ × ___ = ___
___ / ___ = ___
___ / ___ = ___

✂ [5] [25] [5]

___ × ___ = ___
___ × ___ = ___
___ / ___ = ___
___ / ___ = ___

36.2 Multiplication Fact Families

Name: _____ Date: _____

Build Array City

Find two medium-sized boxes (such as tissue boxes). Cut out the windows on this page. You can color the windows if you want! Then glue the windows to the front of your boxes to make the arrays in the lesson. Use your boxes to fill out the repeated addition and multiplication sentences.

4 tall, 3 across

__ + __ + __ + __ = __

__ × __ = __

5 tall, 5 across

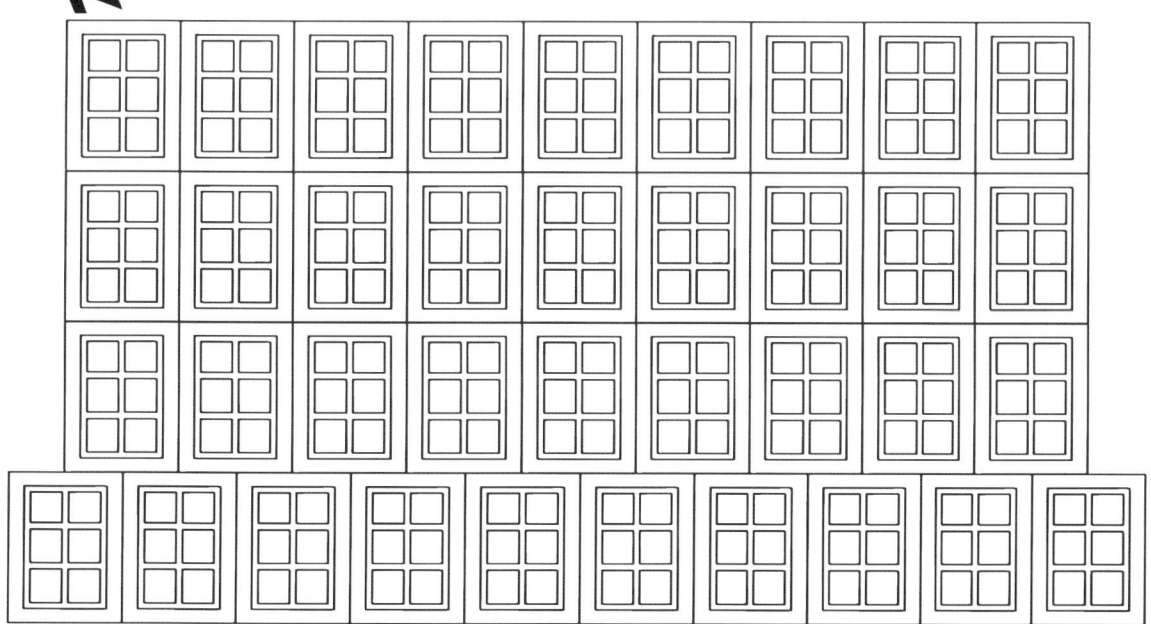

__ + __ + __ + __ + __ = __

__ × __ = __

36.3 Array City

Name: _____ Date: _____

Multiplication Word Problems

Read each word problem. Use highlighters to find the key words and numbers. Glue the correct multiplication sentence under each problem. Then find the answers!

Layla brought 5 bags with 4 stickers in each bag. How many stickers are there in all?

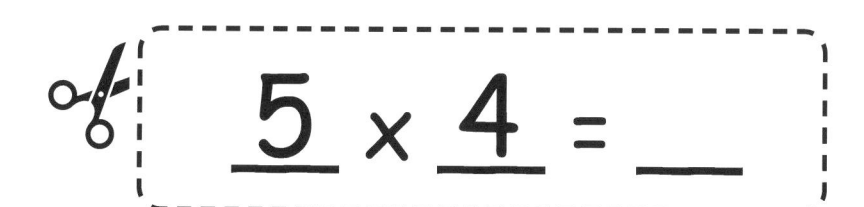

Jayce bought 6 packs of 3 cookies. How many cookies did he bring in total?

✂ $\underline{5} \times \underline{4} = \underline{}$

$\underline{6} \times \underline{3} = \underline{}$

Name: _____ Date: _____

Summer Seed Multiplication

Read the word problems. Highlight the key words in one color. Highlight the numbers in another color. Cut out and glue the numbers to show the correct factors. Write the products on the lines.

Aria has 6 rows of 3 seeds. How many total seeds does she have?

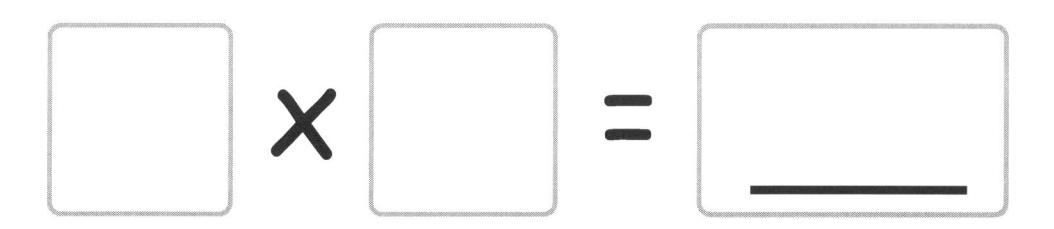

☐ × ☐ = ☐ ____

Aria has 5 bags with 4 seeds in each bag. How many seeds does she have in all?

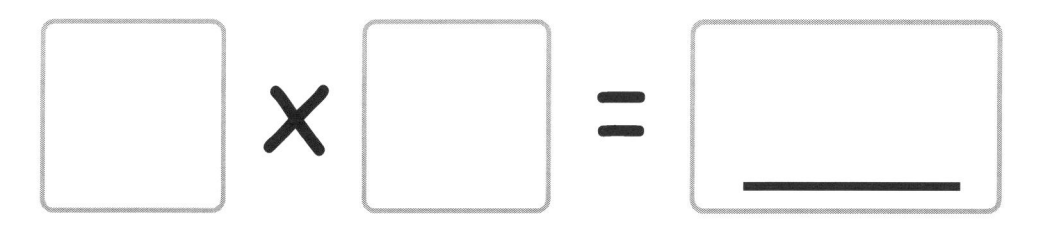

☐ × ☐ = ☐ ____

✂ 3　4　5　6

36.5 Write to Solve

288

Extra Resources

The following pages are extra copies of tools you have learned to use in class. They may be helpful as you work through lessons.

Name: _____ Date: _____

Hundred Chart
Use this hundred chart to find the number.

100

1	2	3	4	5	6	7	8	9	10
11	12	13	14	15	16	17	18	19	20
21	22	23	24	25	26	27	28	29	30
31	32	33	34	35	36	37	38	39	40
41	42	43	44	45	46	47	48	49	50
51	52	53	54	55	56	57	58	59	60
61	62	63	64	65	66	67	68	69	70
71	72	73	74	75	76	77	78	79	80
81	82	83	84	85	86	87	88	89	90
91	92	93	94	95	96	97	98	99	100

Hundred Chart

Name: _____ Date: _____

Hundred Chart
Use this hundred chart to find the number.

100

1	2	3	4	5	6	7	8	9	10
11	12	13	14	15	16	17	18	19	20
21	22	23	24	25	26	27	28	29	30
31	32	33	34	35	36	37	38	39	40
41	42	43	44	45	46	47	48	49	50
51	52	53	54	55	56	57	58	59	60
61	62	63	64	65	66	67	68	69	70
71	72	73	74	75	76	77	78	79	80
81	82	83	84	85	86	87	88	89	90
91	92	93	94	95	96	97	98	99	100

Name: _____ Date: _____

Thousand Chart

Use the number patterns on this chart to count by 100s!

1000

10	20	30	40	50	60	70	80	90	100
110	120	130	140	150	160	170	180	190	200
210	220	230	240	250	260	270	280	290	300
310	320	330	340	350	360	370	380	390	400
410	420	430	440	450	460	470	480	490	500
510	520	530	540	550	560	570	580	590	600
610	620	630	640	650	660	670	680	690	700
710	720	730	740	750	760	770	780	790	800
810	820	830	840	850	860	870	880	890	900
910	920	930	940	950	960	970	980	990	1000

Name: _____ Date: _____

Thousand Chart

Use the number patterns on this chart to count by 100s!

1000

10	20	30	40	50	60	70	80	90	100
110	120	130	140	150	160	170	180	190	200
210	220	230	240	250	260	270	280	290	300
310	320	330	340	350	360	370	380	390	400
410	420	430	440	450	460	470	480	490	500
510	520	530	540	550	560	570	580	590	600
610	620	630	640	650	660	670	680	690	700
710	720	730	740	750	760	770	780	790	800
810	820	830	840	850	860	870	880	890	900
910	920	930	940	950	960	970	980	990	1000

Thousand Chart